TABLE OF CONTENTS

TITLE	STAR	PAGE
A Healthy Pace	Builda	1
Be a Buddy, Not a Bully	Harvest	33
Beaker's Winter Wonders	Beaker	65
Builda the Re-Bicycler	Builda	97
Last but Not Least	Sew	129
Mind Your Manners	Beaker	161
Seasons of the Great Tree	Nueva	193
Seed Day	Brick	225
The Perfect Dress	Sew	257
The Pride of Midlandia	Badge	289
Wilda's General Store Adventure	Wilda	321

Welcome to Midlandia!

A Healthy Pace

A Tales of Midlandia Storybook

by Michael Scotto
illustrated by The Ink Circle

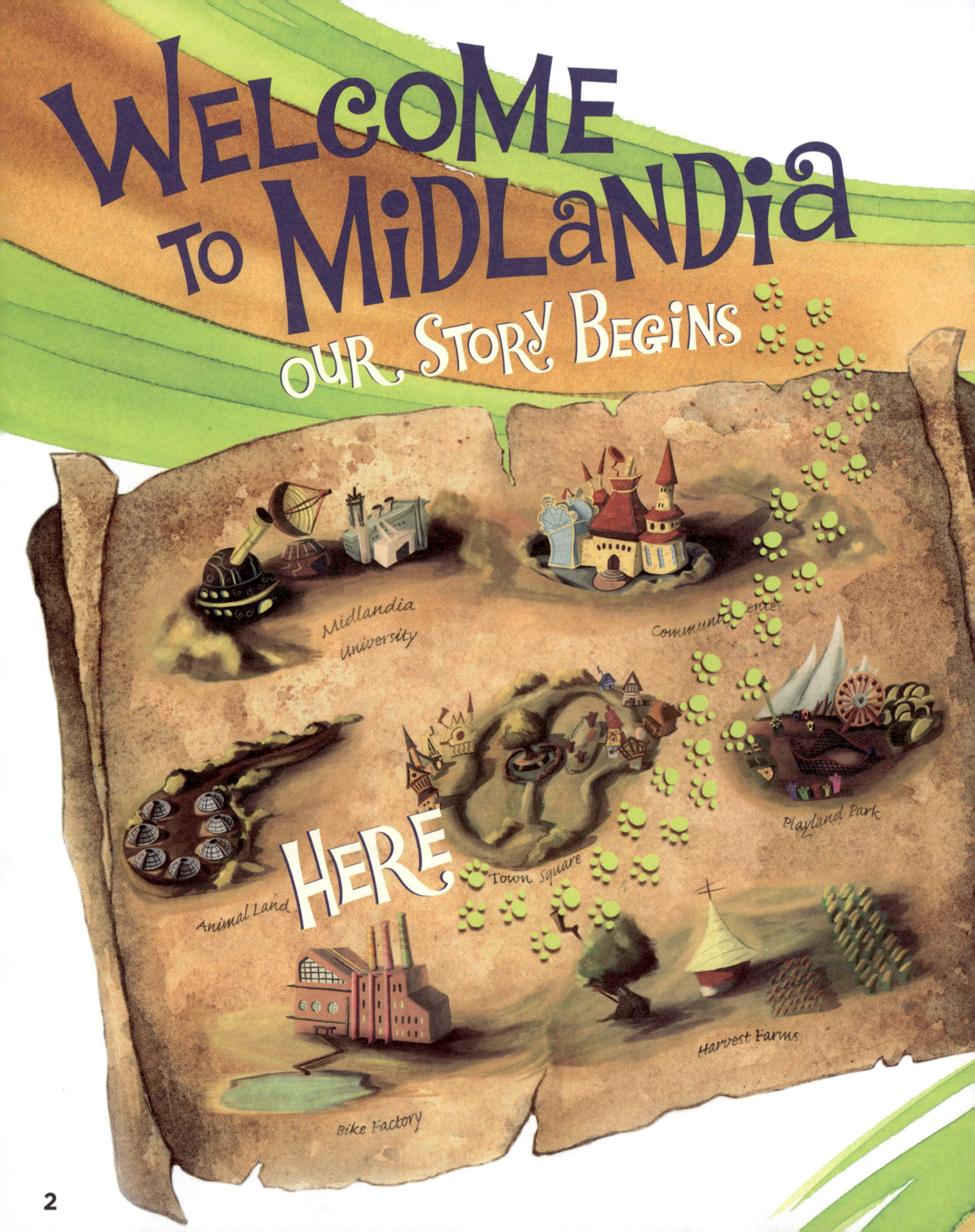

A Healthy Pace

by Michael Scotto
illustrated by The Ink Circle

Once a year, the Midlandians held a bicycle race. It went between the mountains, through the forest, and over the rivers. The race was called the Tour de Midlandia.

Builda had won the race every year since it was first held.

She loved to tell everyone about what a good rider she was. "I've broken every record in the books!" Builda declared.

Builda was quick about everything. She worked quickly, thought quickly, and even ate quickly. She expected everything around her to be quick, too.

"**There you are!**" Builda cried. She had been waiting all morning for Posta to arrive with her new bicycle parts. Posta delivered the mail in Midlandia.

"How can I keep on schedule if everyone else is so slow?" Builda asked.

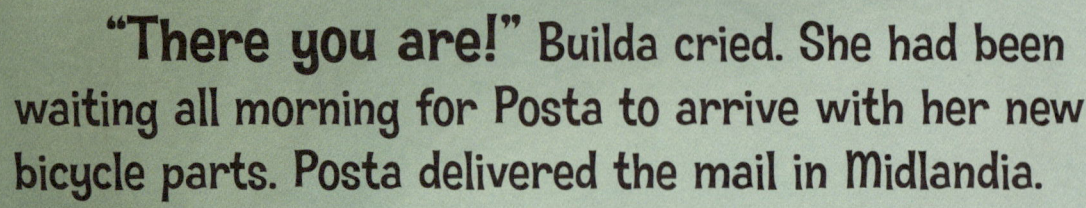

"**I'm sorry,**" Posta told her. "I had a lot of stops to make along the way."

"I guess that you are just a **slowpoke**, then," Builda said. "If I had your job, I'd be so quick that the mail would be delivered before it even got sent out!"

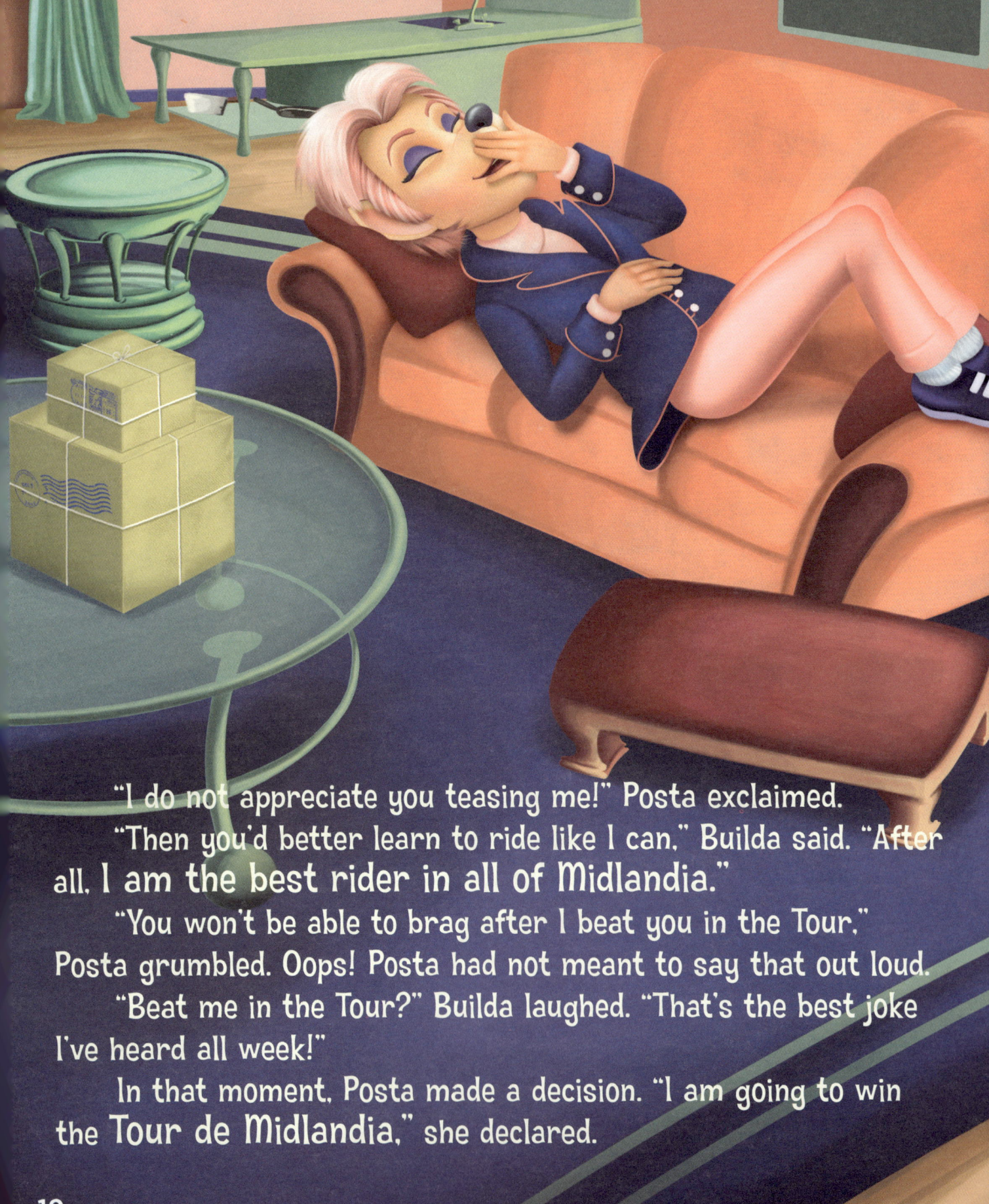

"I do not appreciate you teasing me!" Posta exclaimed.

"Then you'd better learn to ride like I can," Builda said. "After all, I am the best rider in all of Midlandia."

"You won't be able to brag after I beat you in the Tour," Posta grumbled. Oops! Posta had not meant to say that out loud.

"Beat me in the Tour?" Builda laughed. "That's the best joke I've heard all week!"

In that moment, Posta made a decision. "I am going to win the Tour de Midlandia," she declared.

But as she rode away, Posta began to worry. *Builda may brag a lot,* Posta thought, *but she really is the quickest rider around. I'll need some help.*

"Thanks for helping me, Coach," Posta said. Coach marched back and forth in front of her.

"We have a lot of work ahead of us, Posta," he said in his gruff voice. "But as long as you keep at it, getting in better shape is easy."

Coach rode in Posta's sidecar as she pedaled around Midlandia. "You need to be active at least an hour a day," Coach said. "That way, your heart and lungs will be **strong, strong, strong.**"

Coach and Posta did other exercises, too. **"Gallop like a horse!"** Coach said, and they galloped to make their legs strong.

"Do the kangaroo!" he said, and they hopped all the way across the playground.

"**Slither like a snake!**" he said, and they slid to make their bellies strong.

While Posta trained with Coach, Builda spent time at her bicycle factory. *I don't need to practice,* Builda thought. *I'm already quick enough. All that matters is that my bike is nice and shiny for the finish line.*

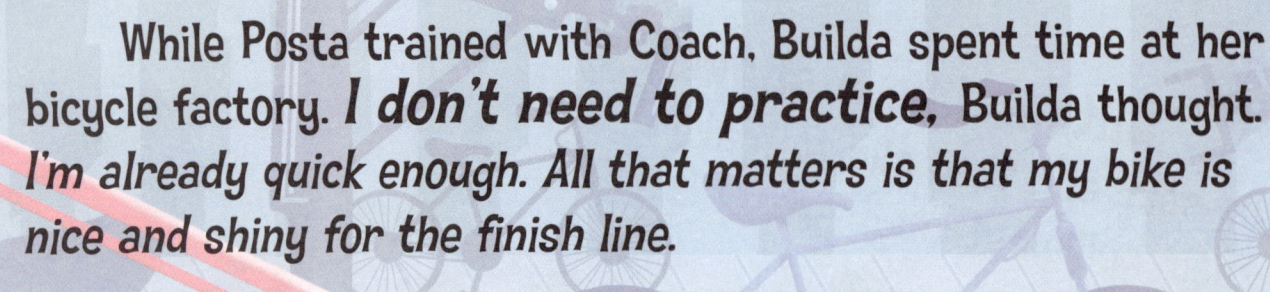

After a week of training, Posta didn't feel **strong, strong, strong**. "I feel **tired, tired, tired**," she said.

"We've been working your muscles too hard," Coach said. "It's good to be strong, but there are other things to think about, too. So, I've brought you to meet my friend, **Sensei!**"

Sensei sat with Posta. "Builda is very fast," he said. "But the key to being healthy is not just being quick. You must be able to **keep a healthy pace.** Allow me to show you how."

Sensei taught Posta new ways to be healthy. First, they ate a snack together. "You should eat healthful foods," Sensei said. "When you are kind to your body, your body is kind to you."

Posta held her arms and legs out. "This seems a little weird," she told Sensei.

"It's good to do different kinds of stretches," he replied. "They help warm your muscles up and keep them from getting too tired."

Soon, it was race day. *I'm going to wear every one of my medals,* Builda thought as she got dressed. *When Posta sees them, she'll really be nervous!*

Builda and Posta arrived at the starting line. While Builda showed off her bike and shiny medals, Posta thought about the things Coach and Sensei had taught her.

"Do not worry if Builda pulls ahead for a little while," they said. **"Just keep a healthy pace."**

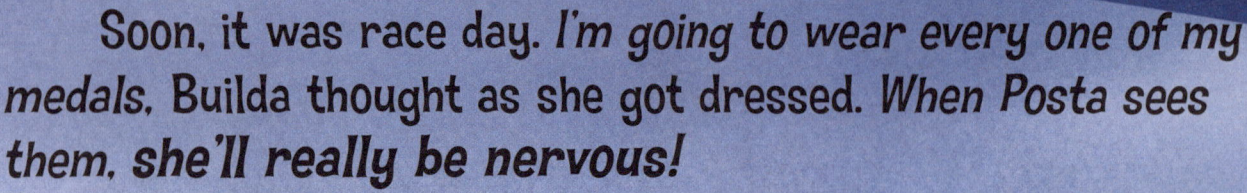

At the starting line, Coach blew his whistle. The riders were off!

Builda pedaled in a burst until she pulled ahead of the pack. "These medals are heavier than I thought they'd be," she huffed, out of breath. Then, Builda saw one rider catching up in the distance. It was Posta!

Keep a healthy pace, Posta thought.

"**I can't let Posta win!**" Builda declared, and she pedaled off as hard as she could.

Builda kept ahead of Posta, but she could never get very far. Builda would pedal very quickly until she got tired and had to slow down. Then, Posta would catch up.

Keep a healthy pace, Posta thought.

By the end of the day, the finish line was in sight.
"I have...to ride...faster," Builda gasped. Posta was still right behind her! Builda pushed and pushed, but her muscles were too worn out. Posta breezed by her and crossed the finish line.

As Coach gave Posta her medal, Builda finally crossed the finish line. "I can't believe it!" she said, her medals clanking together. "**You beat me!**"

"You tired yourself out showing off," Posta told Builda. "That's just not healthy. Like Coach and Sensei told me, **a healthy pace will win the race.**"

Discussion Questions

Why did Builda's behavior at the beginning of the story make Posta upset?

What activities do you like to do for exercise?

A HEALTHY PACE

Revised edition. First printing, January 2008.
Copyright 2021 © Lincoln Learning Solutions. All rights reserved.
294 Massachusetts Avenue
Rochester, PA 15074
Visit us on the web at http://www.lincolnlearningsolutions.org.
Midlandia® is a registered trademark of Lincoln Learning Solutions.

Edited by Ashley Mortimer
Character design by Evette Gabriel
Environmental design by Joshua Perry

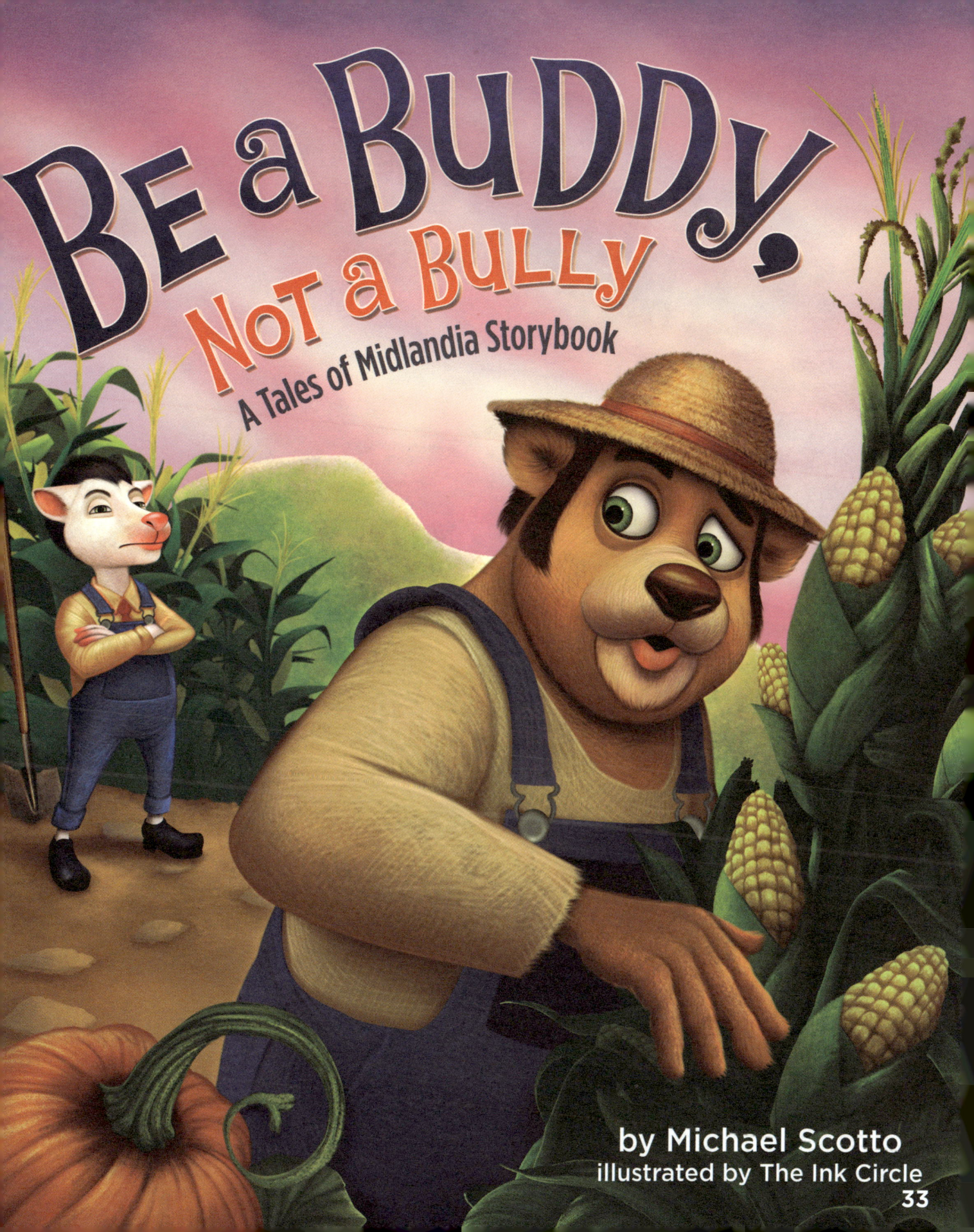

Be a Buddy, Not a Bully

by Michael Scotto
illustrated by The Ink Circle

At the end of a hard day on the farm, Harvest liked to sit by the fire and write in his journal. One evening, Harvest heard a noise outside his window.

It was Buck, the town banker! He was digging away with a shovel at the edge of Harvest's cornfield.

"What are you doing here?" asked Harvest.

"Oh, nothing..." replied Buck. "I'm just seeing if my shovel works."

"But why aren't you trying it in your own yard?" asked Harvest. "And why are you dressed like that?"

"Okay, okay, Harvest. I'll tell you what I'm up to." Buck leaned in very close. "But only if you promise to keep it a secret."

"I promise," said Harvest.

"I'm digging for treasure!" Buck declared, and he jammed his shovel in the dirt.

Harvest put his hands on his belly and laughed. "There's no treasure here!" he said.

Buck shook his head and told Harvest, "This map says otherwise."

"I was digging for treasure at the bottom of the river today when I found this map tucked inside a bottle."

"I don't know about any treasure," said Harvest. "This is just where I plant my ears of corn!"

"Then..." Buck clapped his hands, "I'll just keep digging and let you know if I find anything."

"It doesn't matter what the map says," Harvest insisted. "You can't dig here. This is my land. It belongs to me and my vegetables."

"I'll tell you what," said Buck, raising his eyebrows. "You let me dig on your land...or I'll tell everyone at the market that your vegetables are rotten."

Harvest quickly covered the ears of corn. **"Shh, they'll hear you!"**

Buck squinted his eyes and threw a tantrum, **stomping** his feet and **hurling** ears of corn at Harvest.

"**Stop that!**" cried Harvest. "Why are you being so mean to me?"

"I wouldn't have to be mean if you'd let me do what I want!" hollered Buck.

"I don't want to fight," said Harvest. "I'm going to bed, and I want you to please go home."

"**You're a real spoilsport!**" shouted Buck.

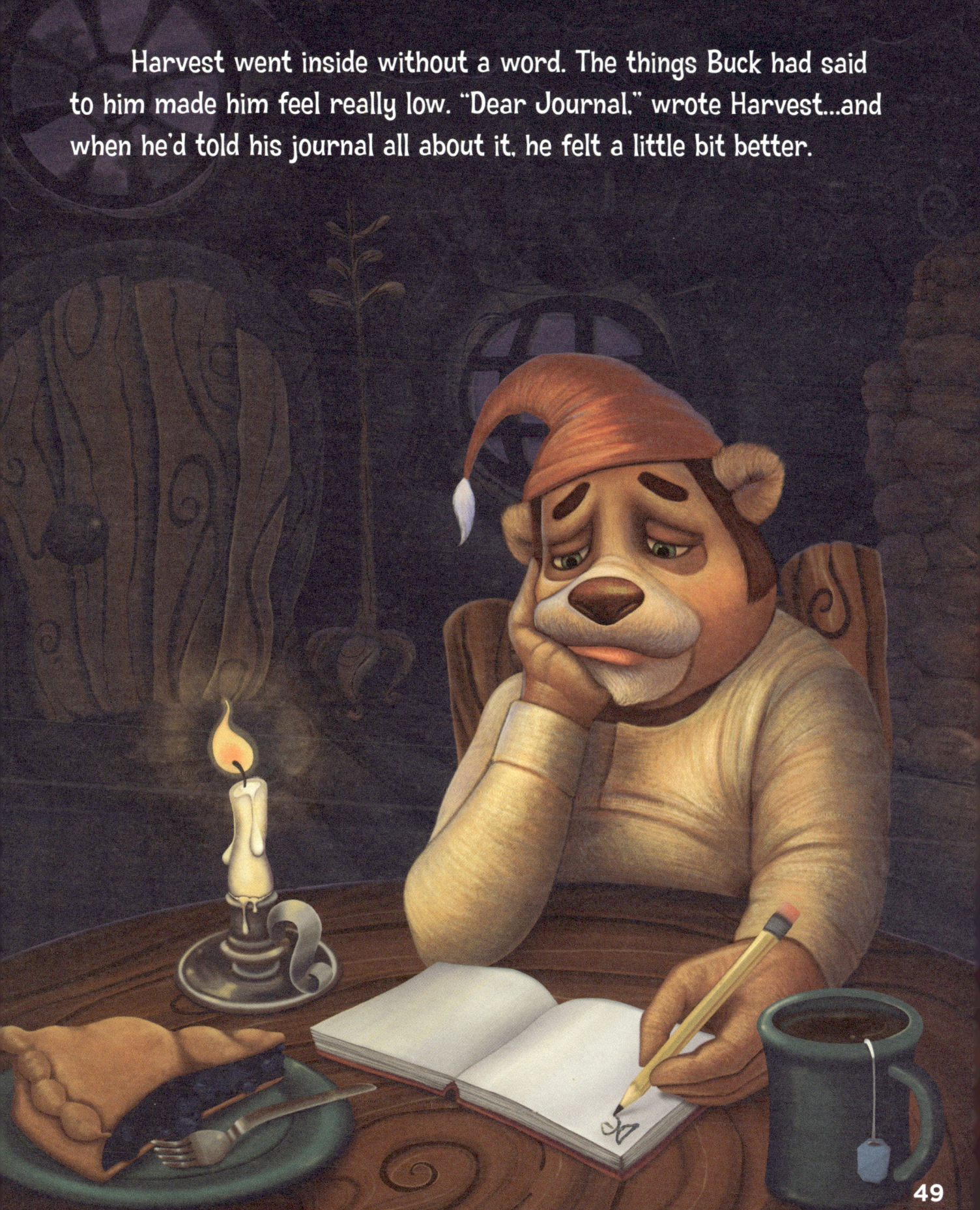

Harvest went inside without a word. The things Buck had said to him made him feel really low. "Dear Journal," wrote Harvest...and when he'd told his journal all about it, he felt a little bit better.

In the morning, Harvest was ready to take some vegetables to the market. But when he got outside, Buck was still digging as if nothing had happened.

"I asked you politely to stop digging on my land," said Harvest. "Now we're going to have a little talk with Chief Tatupu."

"You said you'd keep it all a secret!" cried Buck. "You need to stop being such a sourpuss!"

Harvest stood tall. "And you need to stop calling people names. Let's go."

Buck let out a gulp...

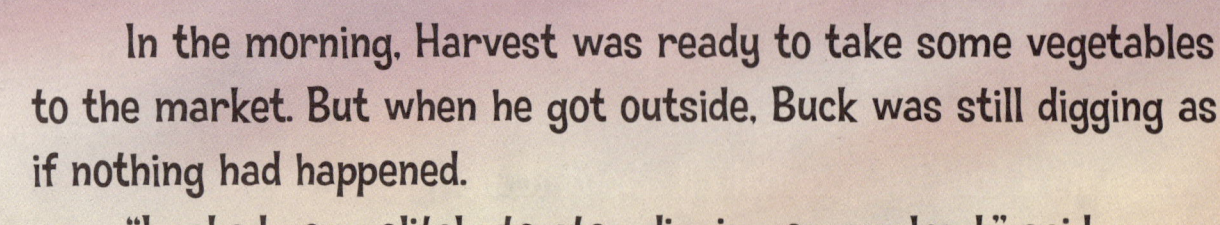

...and off they went.

"What can I do for you two?" asked Chief Tatupu, the leader of Midlandia.

"He won't let me dig for treasure!" complained Buck.

"Buck dug holes in my field without even asking," said Harvest. "He was also really mean, hit me with ears of corn, and called me names. I was so upset that I wrote about it in my journal."

Harvest showed Chief Tatupu his journal, in which he had written about how bad Buck had made him feel.

Chief read the journal. "Buck," he said with a sigh, "this is not a good way to make friends. You should be a buddy, not a bully. Harvest, may I show Buck what you wrote?"

Harvest nodded, and Chief handed Buck the journal. "Read this," Chief said, "and then spend a little time by yourself to think about how you have behaved."

Buck went off to read.

When Harvest and Chief were alone, Harvest said, "I feel awful. What did I do to make Buck bully me?"

"When someone bullies you," explained Chief, "it is not your fault. It is the bully's fault."

Soon, Buck returned to Chief and Harvest. "What do you have to say?" asked Chief.

Buck looked shyly at Harvest. "Harvest, I didn't realize I was hurting your feelings by ordering you around. It was wrong of me to bully you, and **I'm sorry.** Can you forgive me?"

"**I forgive you**," replied Harvest. "And as long as you don't disturb my vegetables, you can look for your buried treasure."

Buck was amazed. "Really?" he asked.

"Sure!" said Harvest. "When Midlandians are kind to me, I always try to be kind to them."

Harvest led Buck back to the farm and fixed them a dinner of mashed potatoes and corn on the cob. When the meal was done, Buck went back to digging, while Harvest wrote about the day in his journal.

Discussion Questions

What does it mean to be a bully? Why is bullying wrong?

What should you do if someone bullies you?

BE A BUDDY, NOT A BULLY

Revised edition. First printing, January 2012.
Copyright 2021 © Lincoln Learning Solutions. All rights reserved.
294 Massachusetts Avenue
Rochester, PA 15074
Visit us on the web at http://www.lincolnlearningsolutions.org.
Midlandia® is a registered trademark of Lincoln Learning Solutions.

Edited by Ashley Mortimer
Great Tree concept art by Matthew Casper

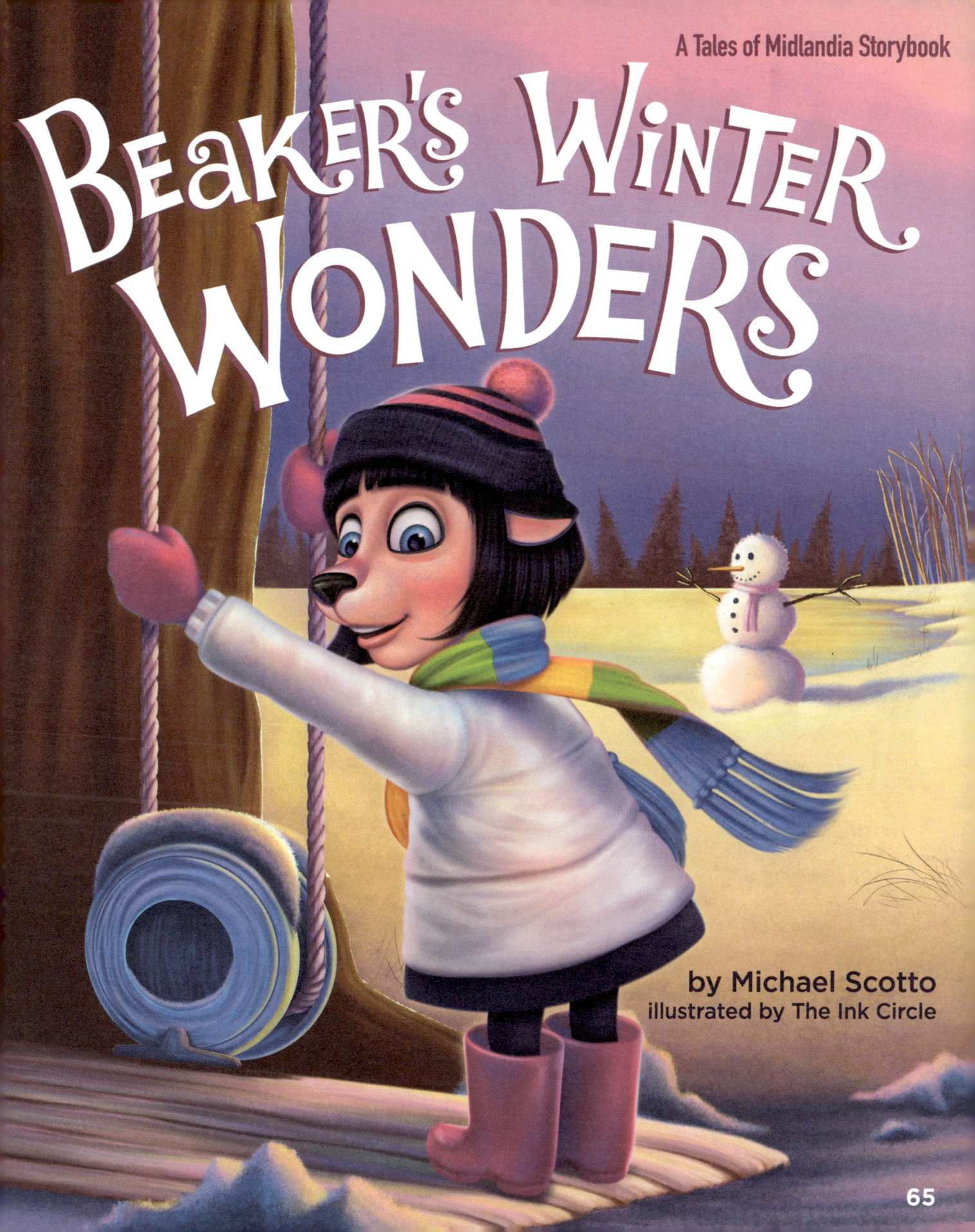

Beaker's Winter Wonders

A Tales of Midlandia Storybook

by Michael Scotto
illustrated by The Ink Circle

Welcome to Midlandia

Our Story Begins

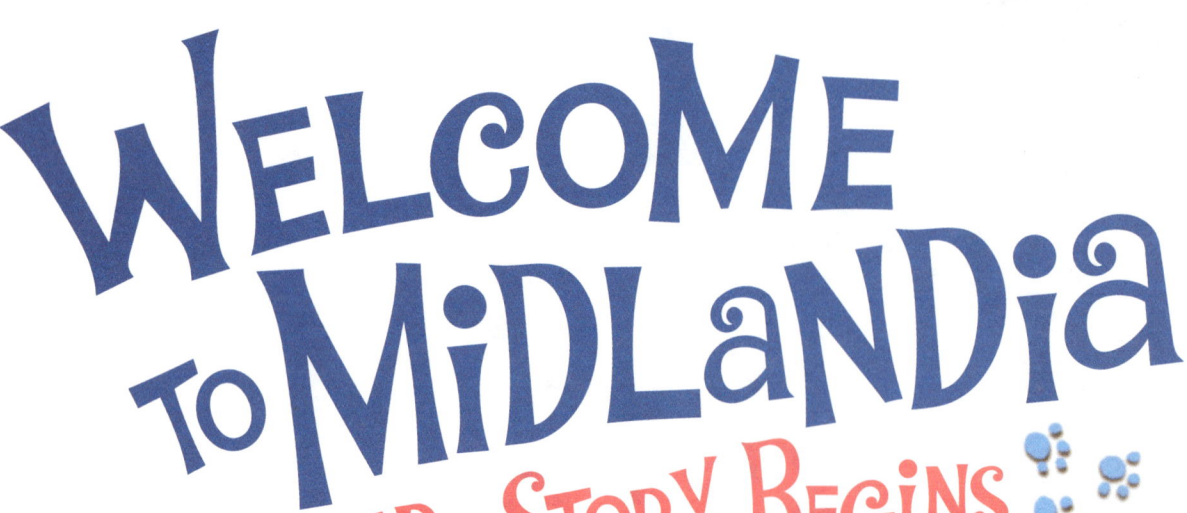

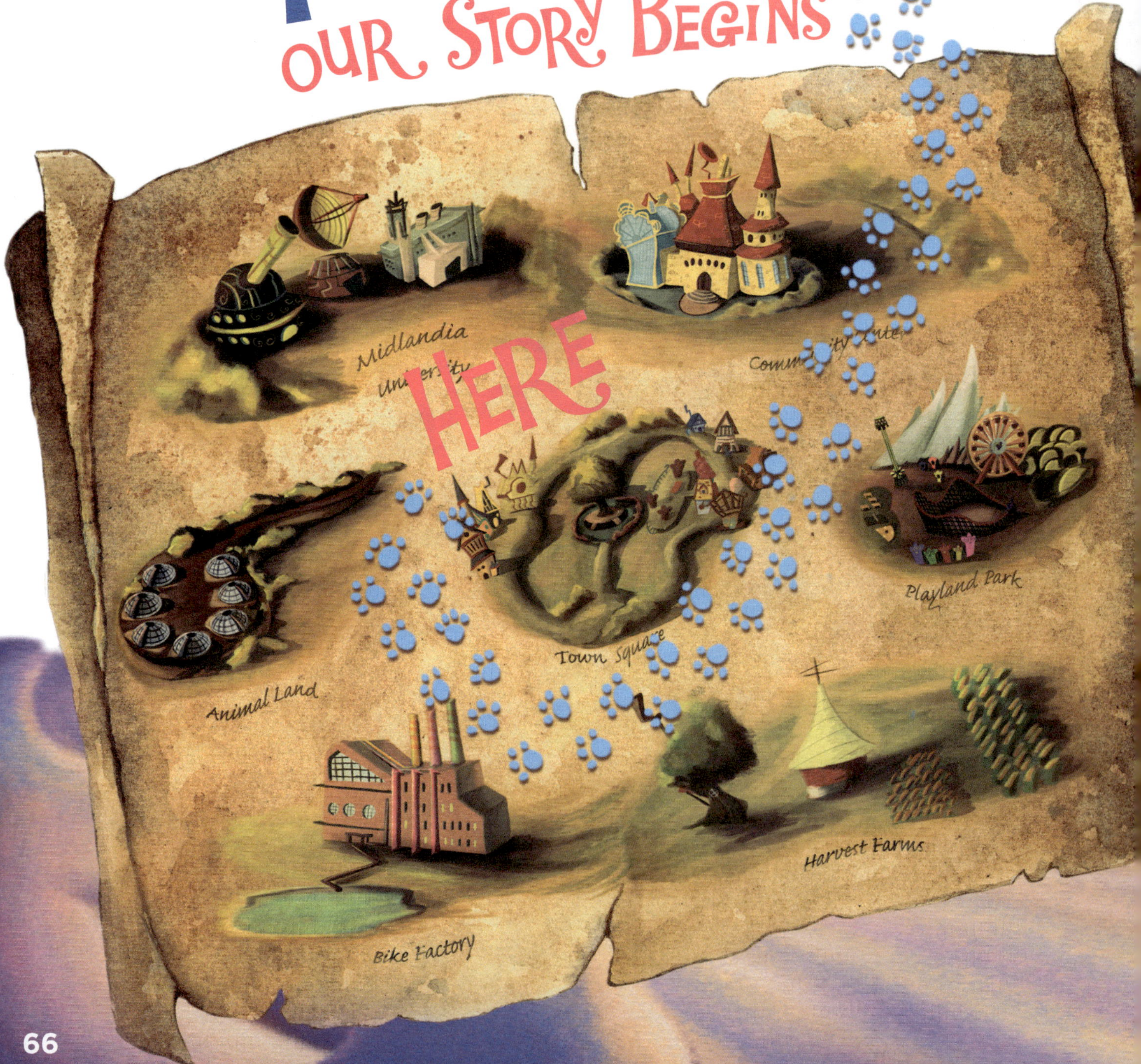

Beaker's Winter Wonders

by Michael Scotto
illustrated by The Ink Circle

"I wonder...." That was Beaker's favorite way to start a sentence. Everything she saw made her curious.

Luckily, it was Beaker's job to be curious. She was a scientist. A scientist works to answer questions about the world. When a scientist sees something that makes them wonder, they try to learn more about it.

Year-round, Beaker wandered about Midlandia and wondered about its mysteries. In spring, "**I wonder** why cardinals sing."

In fall, "**I wonder** why blueberries are blue."

Even in summer, "**I wonder** why sand gets so hot in the sunshine. **Yowch!**"

But Beaker looked forward to winter the most. When the snow began to fall, Midlandia became a regular wonderland.

"It all looks so different!" said Beaker. "I **wonder** how much snow is on the ground!"

Beaker bundled up in her warmest clothes. Then, she lowered herself from her house for a long, wandering, wondering walk.

I wonder why ice floats, thought Beaker. *I wonder* how snowballs stick together.

But as Beaker wandered (and wondered), she noticed something odd. *The woods seem so quiet today,* she thought. ***I wonder why.***

Beaker studied the trees and their bare branches. Then, it hit her.

"All the birds are gone!" cried Beaker. Her question was answered. But now she had a new mystery.

"**I wonder** where they went!"

Just like that, Beaker was on the hunt. But where to start?

"Maybe the birds went to get some food," she guessed.

Beaker scurried all through the bakery. She searched the kitchen.

She peeked under the tables.

She even checked in Bun the baker's hat. "Excuse me!" said Bun. But Beaker found no birds. "Maybe they went somewhere to warm their wings," she guessed.

Beaker knocked on every door in Tree Town, where most Midlandians lived. Some Midlandians were not very polite.

"Got any birds in there?" asked Beaker.

"What do you think this is?" snapped Buck. **"A zoo?"**

"**The zoo!**" Beaker said as she plowed through the snow. "I completely forgot to look there."

The Animal Land zoo had lots of birds from all over the world. They lived in a special home called an aviary. The aviary was warm all year and had lots of room for flying.

I'll bet all the forest birds moved in there, thought Beaker.

In the aviary, Beaker saw many birds. But there were no robins, blue jays, or woodpeckers.

Beaker grew worried. "Where are the birds from the forest?" she wondered aloud.

Then, the strangest thing happened. One of the birds spoke back! It was a parrot.

"**Hello,**" he said.

Soon, it was dinnertime at Animal Land. Wilda, the zookeeper, had a bucket of seeds and fruit ready for the birds. When Wilda reached the aviary, she spotted Beaker with the parrot. *What on earth is she doing?* thought Wilda.

Beaker was trying to get some answers about the missing birds. "Do you know where they went?" she asked.

"Hello," said the parrot.
"If you tell me," replied Beaker,
"I'll give you free crackers for life!"
"Hello," said the parrot.

"What's going on here?" asked Wilda.
Beaker was very frustrated. "The birds in the forest have gone missing!" she exclaimed. "I think this bird knows something about it. **But he is being very stubborn!**"

Wilda smiled. "That parrot probably cannot help you," she said. "**But I can.**"

"You know where the birds in the forest went?" asked Beaker.

"**Sure, I do!**" replied Wilda. "The birds in the forest all migrated."

"**Oh, no!**" Beaker wailed. "I'll bet that really hurt."

Wilda shook her head. "When birds migrate, it doesn't hurt," she said. "It just means they moved away for a while."

"They moved away from Midlandia?" asked Beaker, shocked.

"Only for the winter," Wilda explained. "When winter comes, the environment changes. Fruits and nuts stop growing from the trees. The bugs and worms that birds eat go deep underground to keep warm. So, birds migrate for a while to someplace warmer, where they can find food."

"So, my guesses were right after all!" said Beaker. "I was just looking in the wrong places." She turned to the parrot. "I'm sorry for pestering you," she told him.

"Hello," said the parrot.

That night, Beaker walked home. She was very happy to have solved her bird mystery. She still had one question, though.
"**I wonder** how the birds will find their way back in the spring!"

But that was a mystery for another day.

Discussion Questions

When you have a question, what are some ways
you can learn the answer?

In winter, what is the weather like near you?
How is it different from other seasons?
How do you dress in winter?

Have you ever been to the zoo?
What is your favorite zoo animal? Why do you like it?

BEAKER'S WINTER WONDERS

Revised edition. First printing, January 2010.
Copyright 2021 © Lincoln Learning Solutions. All rights reserved.
294 Massachusetts Avenue
Rochester, PA 15074
Visit us on the web at http://www.lincolnlearningsolutions.org.
Midlandia® is a registered trademark of Lincoln Learning Solutions.

Edited by Ashley Mortimer
Character design by Evette Gabriel
Environmental design by Joshua Perry

Builda
The Re-Bicycler

by Michael Scotto
illustrated by The Ink Circle

The town of Midlandia was bicycle-crazy! Every bike in town came from the same place: Builda's factory. She made beautiful bikes, and the Midlandians kept her very busy.

"I have a problem," said Sparky. "My front tire popped." That certainly was a problem. Sparky was a firefighter, and he needed good tires to ride quickly from place to place.

"**Don't worry,**" replied Builda. "I'll have a brand-new bike for you by the end of the week."

It may seem odd to build a brand-new bike when the only problem is a popped tire. But in Midlandia, this was quite common. When any little thing broke on a bike, its owner threw the bike away and bought a new one.

Sometimes, Midlandians threw away bikes that had nothing wrong with them at all.

Every old bike was added to the garbage dump, which was a huge hole in the ground near the edge of town.

"I'm tired of this pink bike," said Beaker as she rolled it into the dump. "I want a blue one."

Throwing away all of these bikes had always seemed like a waste to Builda. *But it is the way things have always been done,* she thought. There had never been a reason to change—until now.

When Builda brought Sparky's bike to the dump, she saw an unusual sight. The dump was full! *No, it's more than full,* thought Builda. **It is overflowing!**

All sorts of mostly good bikes were tangled in a towering pile. "I have to do something about this," she declared.

But what could she do? *If I dig another dump,* thought Builda, *it will just fill up, too. And if we keep on digging dumps, there won't be room for anything else!*

Then, a bike in the dump caught Builda's eye. This bike had a bent frame. "But the tires are fine!" she cried. **Builda had a plan!**

Builda carried both bikes back to her factory and worked through the night. In the morning, she asked Sparky to visit her.

"You made my new bike so quickly!" said Sparky. "**Thank you, Builda.**"

Sparky rode a few test laps around the factory. "It rides just like my old bike," he told Builda with a beaming smile. **"And it looks just like it, too."**

"That's because it is your old bike," said Builda.

Sparky was confused. "My bike was broken," he replied.

"You only had a popped tire," explained Builda. "The rest of your bike was fine. So, I found another bike with a perfect tire, and I put that tire on your bike."

"What a neat idea!" said Sparky. "It saved a lot of time."

"And if we keep reusing our old bike parts," added Builda, "it will also make a lot less garbage."

"You need to tell everyone about your idea," said Sparky. "You could have Vincent make a poster about it for the Town Square."

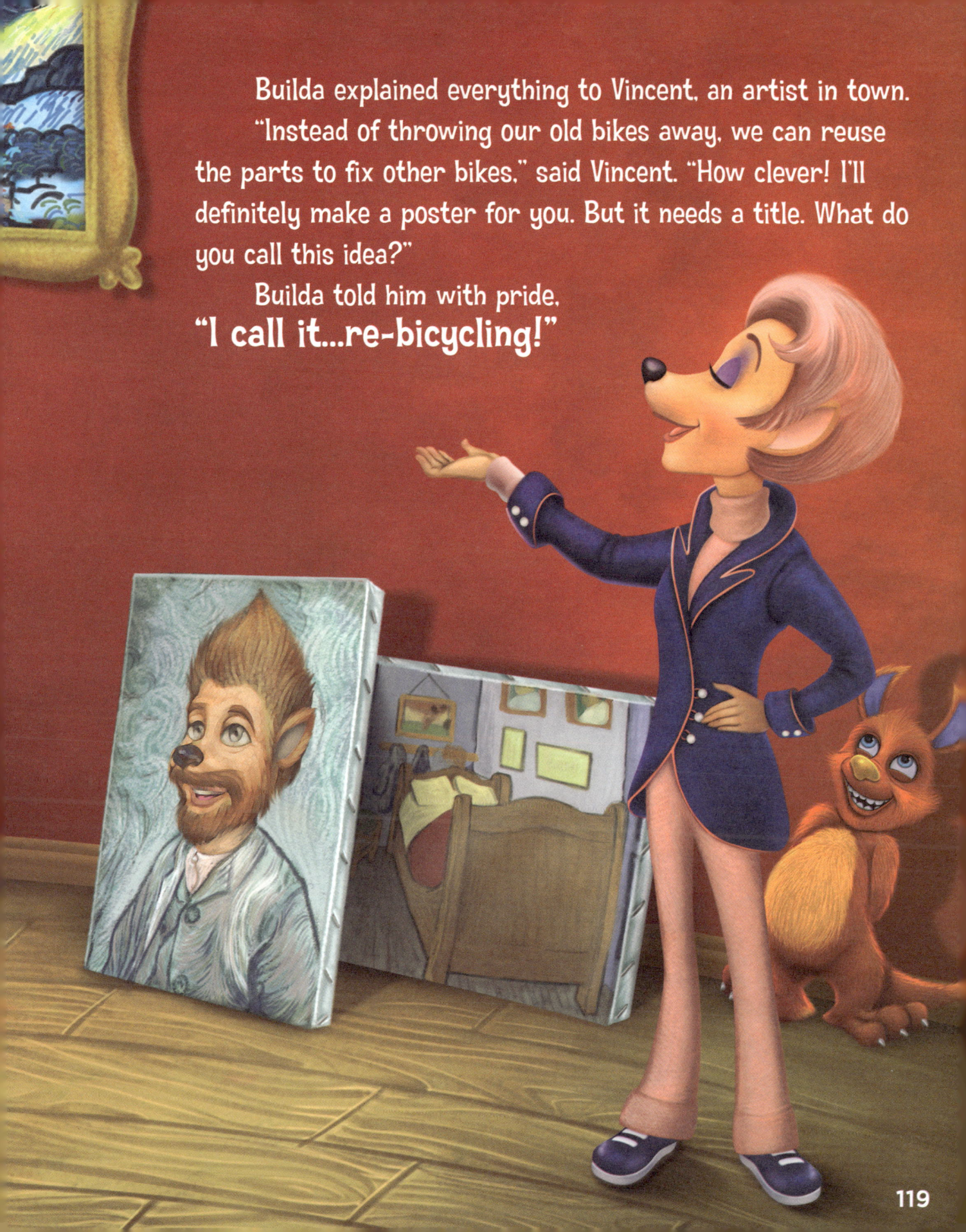

Builda explained everything to Vincent, an artist in town.

"Instead of throwing our old bikes away, we can reuse the parts to fix other bikes," said Vincent. "How clever! I'll definitely make a poster for you. But it needs a title. What do you call this idea?"

Builda told him with pride,
"I call it...re-bicycling!"

While Vincent worked on the poster, Builda rescued as many busted bikes as she could from the dump.

All through the night, she split the good parts from the bad. She kept the good parts that she could reuse and returned the broken ones to the dump.

Builda went to check on Vincent.

"Your poster is almost ready," he said, "but there is one problem. This word—*re-bicycling*—it's too long to fit on the poster. Can we give your idea a shorter name?"

Builda thought long and hard. Finally, she said, "Why don't we call it **recycling**?"

"Brilliant!" said Vincent. "Recycling is a perfect fit."

Vincent was right—recycling was a perfect fit. Soon, Midlandians began using Builda's idea for more than just bikes.

"Instead of throwing our bottles and cans into the dump," said Beaker, "we can recycle them to make new ones!"

"We can take used paper and recycle it to make new paper!" exclaimed Nueva.

After some time, Chief Tatupu, the leader of Midlandia, visited Builda's factory. "**I have wonderful news,**" he said. "For your idea, recycling, I have come to award you with a great honor: the **Spirit of Midlandia trophy!**"

Builda's eyes grew wide. "I don't know if I deserve that," she stammered.

"Recycling has helped us in so many ways," said Chief.

"It's reduced the trash that we produce and helped save our resources," said Sparky.

"But best of all," noted Vincent, "it has made Midlandia a cleaner and more beautiful place."

"All that happened because of my little idea?" asked Builda.

Chief smiled. "We are having a ceremony for you tomorrow evening. I hope you will come."

The whole town **applauded** as Builda accepted her prize. "It is made from recycled material," whispered Chief.
As her community clapped and cheered, Builda realized that sometimes, one little idea can make a huge difference.

Discussion Questions

Name three objects in your home that you can reuse after you are finished with them.

Tell how you would use each object in a different way.

Recycling is a form of community service. Can you think of other ways that you can help your community?

BUILDA THE RE-BICYCLER

Revised edition. First printing, January 2012.
Copyright 2021 © Lincoln Learning Solutions. All rights reserved.
294 Massachusetts Avenue
Rochester, PA 15074
Visit us on the web at http://www.lincolnlearningsolutions.org.
Midlandia® is a registered trademark of Lincoln Learning Solutions.

Edited by Ashley Mortimer
Midlandian Map by Danielle Caruso

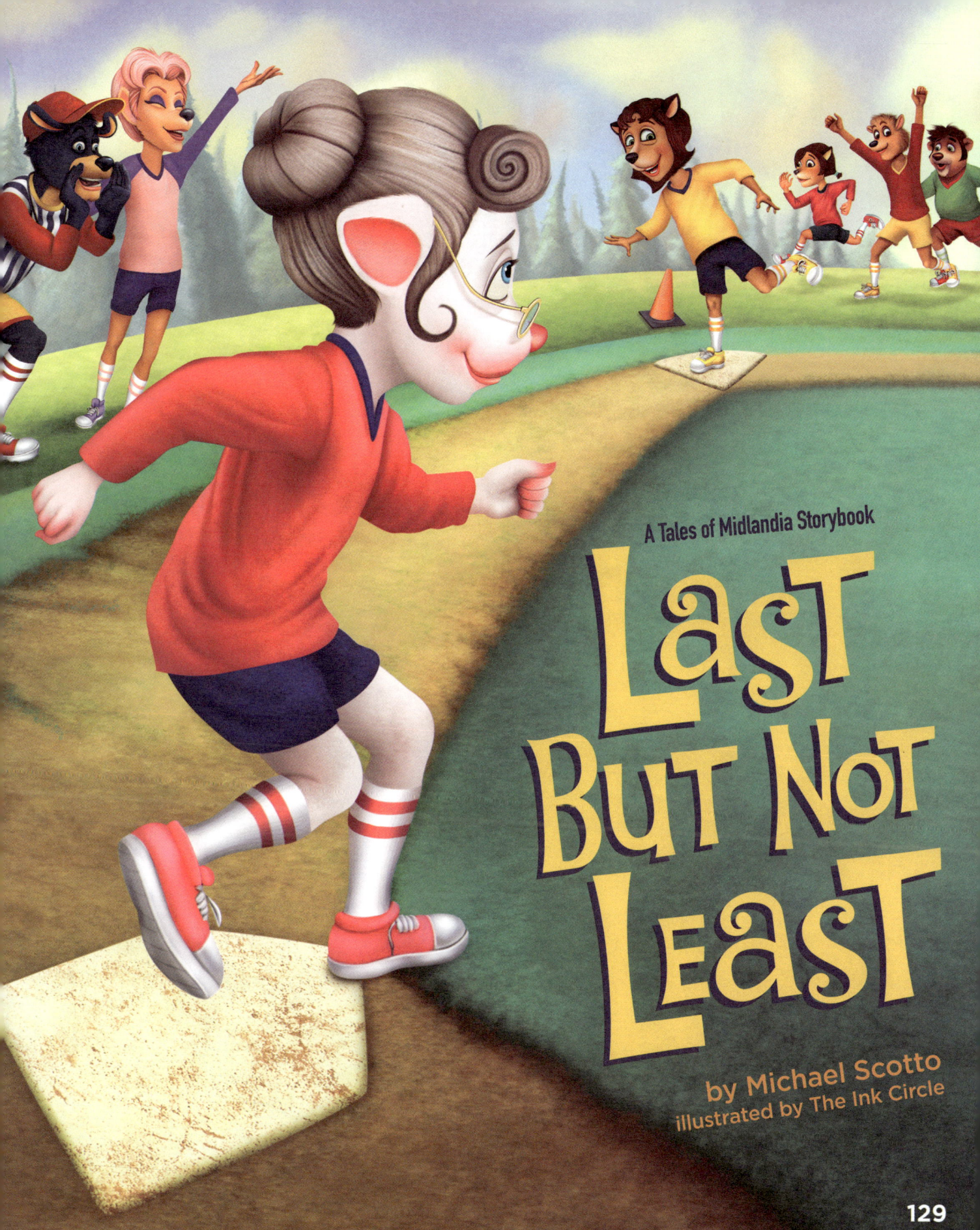

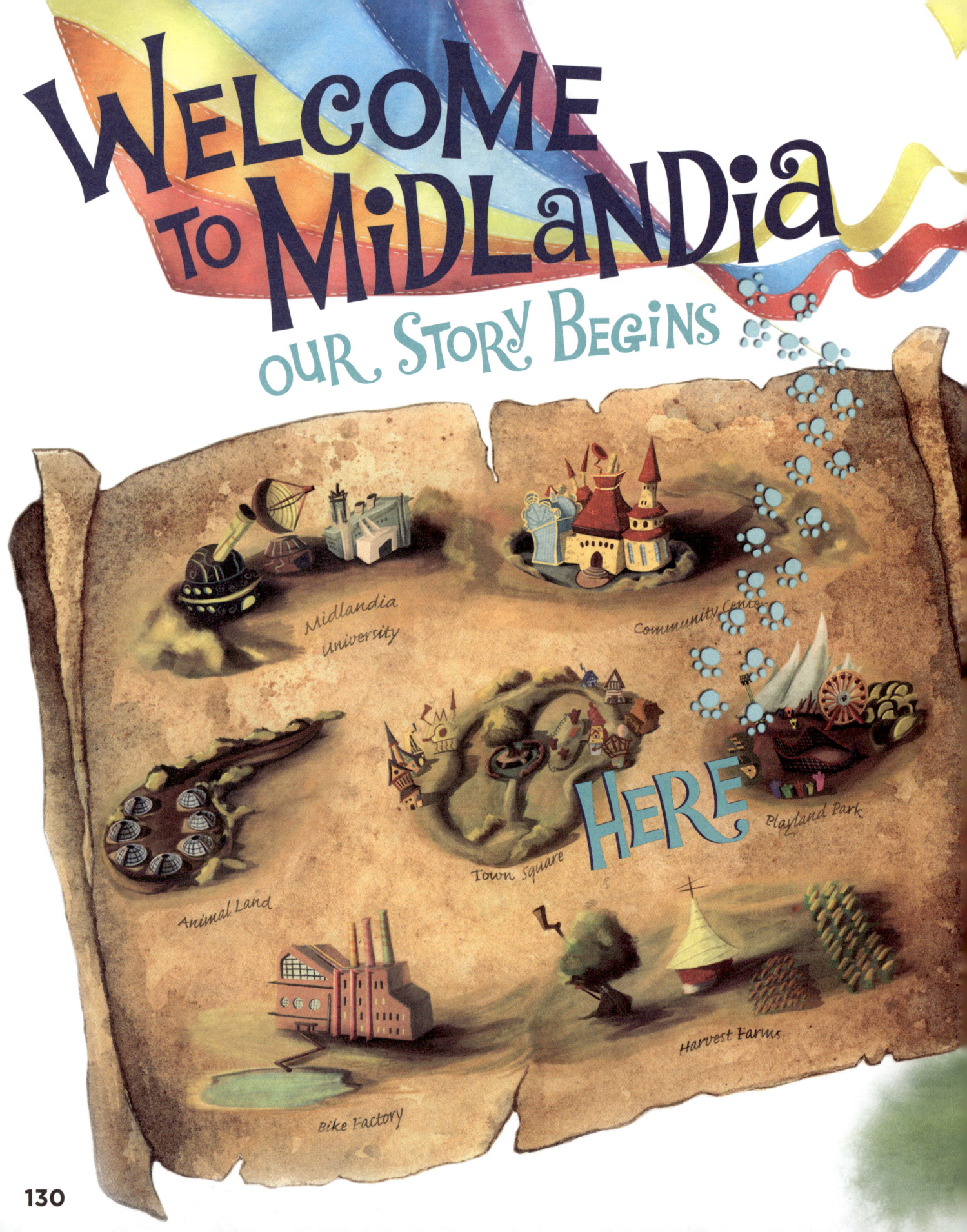

Last But Not Least

by Michael Scotto
illustrated by The Ink Circle

The Midlandia Summer Festival took place every year. Everyone in town got together to enjoy the sun, eat delicious food, and play games.

Sew loved the picnic. *The sky is perfect for kiteflying!* she thought. Sew was a seamstress, and she had a special kite that she had stitched herself.

Sew loved nearly everything about the festival, everything except....
"**The games,**" she grumbled.

It wasn't that Sew did not want to play. She wanted to play very much. *But when we split into teams, I always get picked last,* Sew thought. *Being picked last just isn't any fun.*

Still, Sew was willing to give the games another chance. *After all, Builda is captain of one of the kickball teams,* Sew thought. Builda and Sew had become good friends over the last year. **This time could be different.**

Sew waited with everyone as Builda and Brick picked their teams. "I'll take Sparky," Builda said. "I'll take Harvest," Brick said. **Sew began to get nervous.**

Soon, Sew was standing alone.
"We have seven, and you have six," Brick told Builda. **"So, you have to take Sew."**

Sew smiled. She was the last one picked, but at least she was on her friend's team. Builda looked at Sew. **"Um...that's okay,"** Builda said to Brick. "You go ahead and have one extra."

Sew was shocked! "But Builda..." she started.

"Sorry, Sew," Builda replied. "I know we're buddies, but I play to win."

Coach, the referee, came and blew his whistle. "Builda!" he barked. "You need to have the same number on each team, or you can't play the game. **Go on over, Sew.**"

Brick snickered as Coach jogged away. "Yes!" Brick said. "With Sew on the other team, there's no way we can lose!"
Sew felt very embarrassed.

"All right," Builda told her team. "We can still win this game, even with Sew on our side."

"I'm not that bad, everybody," Sew protested. "I might not be the fastest, or the best thrower—"

"When we played horseshoes last year," Builda interrupted, "you broke every window in the community center!" **The whole team laughed.**

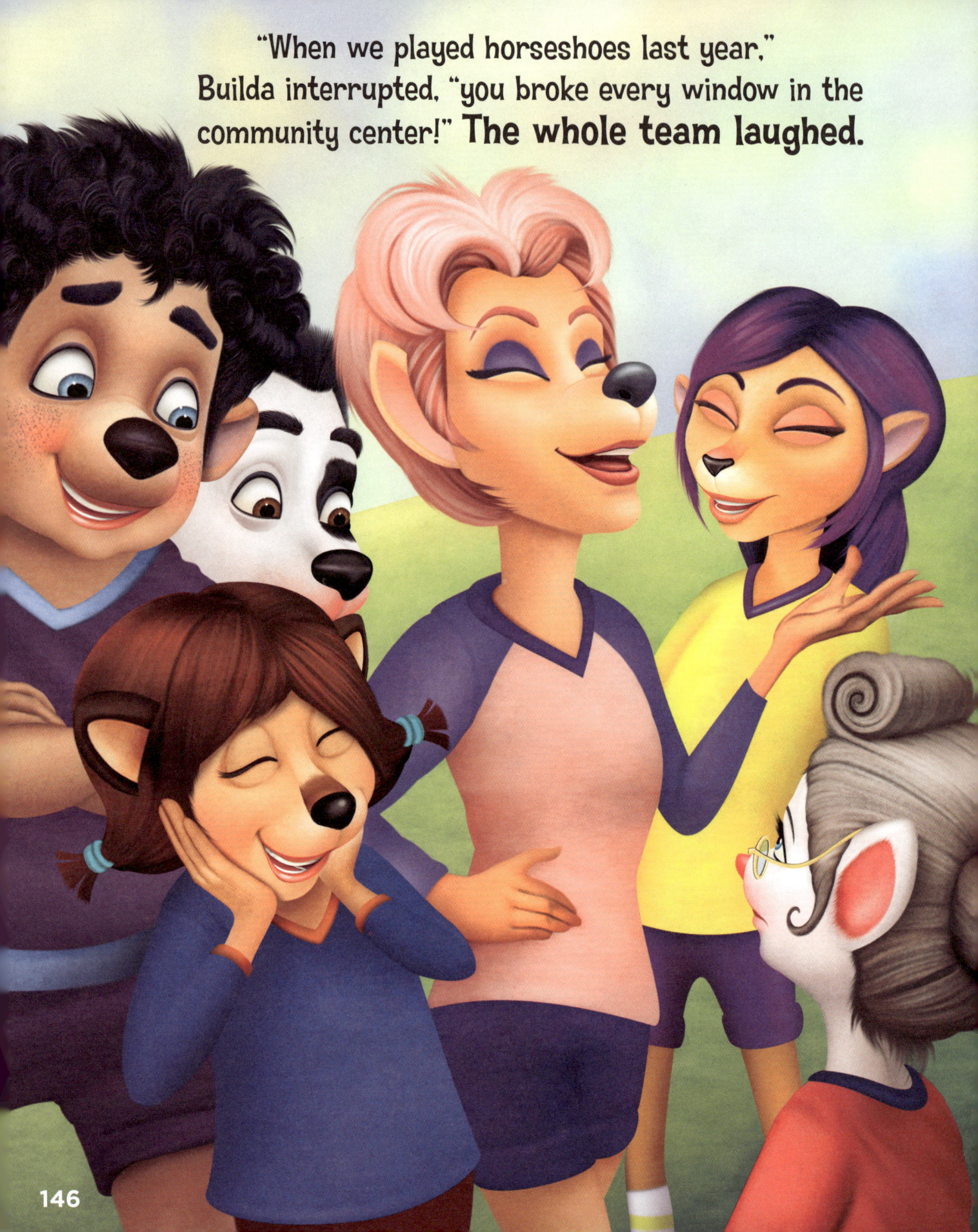

Sew had had enough. "If you're going to laugh at me," she said, "I'll just go fly my kite."

"No, wait!" Builda called out. But Sew had already left the field.

Sew's kite glided through the air. She preferred to fly kites with friends, but everyone else was still at the Summer Festival. *At least I have the sky all to myself,* Sew thought. Then, she heard a voice behind her.

"It must be lonely to fly that kite all alone," Coach said.

"It's better than being laughed at," Sew replied.

Coach sat down beside Sew. "I've already spoken with Builda and everyone else," he said. "They should not have been making fun."

"Yes, they should have!" Sew said. "**I'm terrible at sports.** I never wanted to play anyway."

"Is that really true?" Coach asked.

"No," Sew huffed.

"It's okay if you aren't very good at kickball," Coach said. "That's no reason to stop trying. **Nobody is good at everything.**"

"I don't feel like I'm good at anything, Coach," Sew said. **"I can't run fast...**

...or jump high...

...and when the ball comes to me, I get really nervous and **I miss it."**

"There are plenty of other things you are great at," Coach said. "You sew wonderful clothes. And look up in the sky. You might not be able to jump very high, but the kite you made soars higher than any other in Midlandia."

Sew blushed. "Really?"

"The next time I need a new kite, you'll be the first Midlandian I talk to!" Coach declared.

"**Thanks, Coach,**" Sew said. "That makes me feel better."

"I know getting picked last can hurt your feelings," Coach told Sew. "Just remember that **last does not always mean least.** Do you think you can give kickball another chance?"

Sew returned to the kickball field.

"We're sorry for giving you a hard time," Builda told her.

"It was not very nice of us," Brick added.

"I forgive you," Sew said. **"Let's play ball!"**

Coach blew his whistle and the game began. After everyone had played for a while, it was finally Sew's turn at the plate.

"All right, Sew, you're the last one to kick," Builda said.

Sew was excited to get a chance, but she was nervous, too. *What if I miss the ball and ruin the game?* she thought. Then, Sew spotted Coach on the sidelines.

"**Last is not least!**" he shouted.

Sew knew that **Coach was right**. As Brick rolled the kickball toward her, Sew stopped worrying. She just ran forward and gave the **best kick** she could. As it turned out, Sew's best was more than good enough.

Discussion Questions

In this story, Sew is picked last to play kickball. Was there ever a time you felt left out of an activity?

How did you handle it?

LAST BUT NOT LEAST

Revised edition. First printing, January 2008.
Copyright 2021 © Lincoln Learning Solutions. All rights reserved.
294 Massachusetts Avenue
Rochester, PA 15074
Visit us on the web at http://www.lincolnlearningsolutions.org.
Midlandia® is a registered trademark of Lincoln Learning Solutions.

Edited by Ashley Mortimer
Character design by Evette Gabriel
Environmental design by Joshua Perry

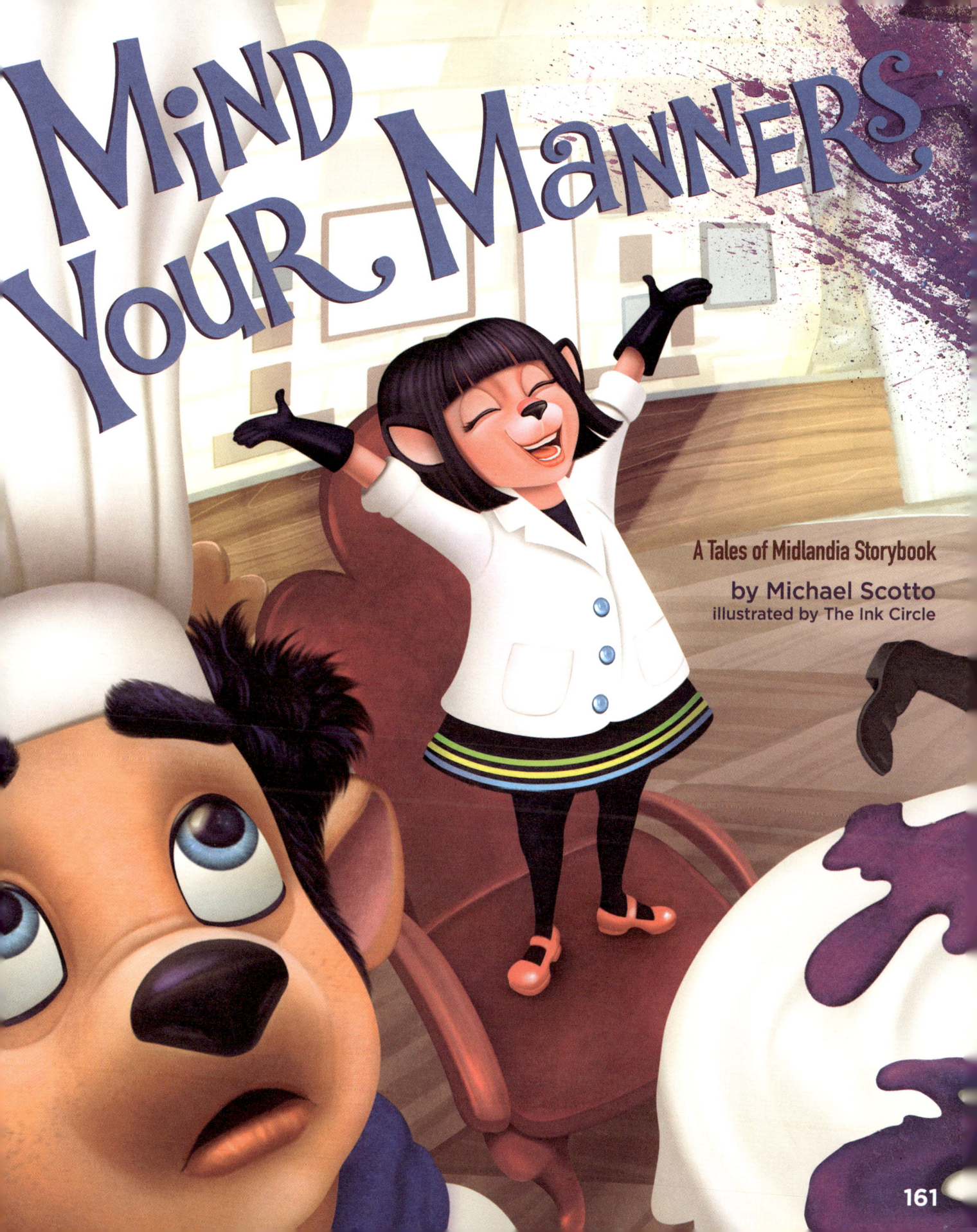

Mind Your Manners

A Tales of Midlandia Storybook
by Michael Scotto
illustrated by The Ink Circle

Mind Your Manners

by Michael Scotto
illustrated by The Ink Circle

Beaker the scientist worked every day in her lab. One Saturday, she heard a knock at the door.

"Posta, how are you today?" Beaker asked.

"I'm just fine," Posta replied. "I have a letter for you."

"For me?" Beaker asked. "I haven't gotten a letter in months!"

Beaker opened the letter and read it to Posta. "We are pleased to announce that you are the winner of the Midlandian Bobel Prize for Science!"

"That's great, Beaker!" Posta cried.

"Science is very important to any community," Beaker read. "To honor your study of the blueberry, we are holding a special banquet at the Town Square on Sunday night. There, you will receive your award."

"**Congratulations!**" Posta said. But Beaker's face became a frown. "What's wrong?" Posta asked.

"I can't go to the banquet," Beaker sighed. "I'm a whiz in the lab, but I never know how to act at fancy dinners. I just don't have good manners."

"You could practice," Posta suggested.

"But the banquet is Sunday night," Beaker said. "That's tomorrow!"

"Then we'd better hurry!" Posta replied.

Beaker zoomed down the road in Posta's mail cart.

"Where are we going?" Beaker asked.

"If you need to learn about manners," Posta answered, "there's only one place to practice." Beaker climbed out of Posta's cart in front of the bakery. "If anyone can help you," Posta said, "it's Bun."

Beaker sat at a table, and Bun swiftly stepped up beside her.

"*Bonjour!* Thank you for choosing the Blueberry Bakery and Bistro. How can I serve you?"

Beaker explained her problem to Bun.

"It's probably not as bad as you think," Bun said. "Let me set this table and get you a pie."

171

In a flash, Bun set up a perfect table for Beaker, with a steaming blueberry pie. "Now," Bun said, "show me how you would eat at a fancy dinner."

Beaker picked up the pie and plunged her face into it.
"Wait, Beaker!" Bun cried.
"This is **scrumptious!**" Beaker said, her face purple. "Try it!"

"That's all right," Bun said. "Really!"

Beaker quickly calculated how far away Bun's mouth was, and she flicked him a big spoonful of pie. The pie flew across the room and landed right on Bun's nose.

"Oops, sorry!" Beaker said. "I guess my numbers were off."

Bun blew the berries out of his nose, only to see Beaker making a mountain out of her blueberry filling. "Beaker, you can't make a mountain out of your food!" Bun said.

"It's not a mountain," Beaker said through a mouthful of pie. **"It's a volcano!"**

177

Beaker's blueberry volcano **exploded** and pelted the entire shop. Bun's other customers shrieked and ran as their clothes were stained **blue** and **purple**.

"That is enough!" Bun cried. "If we practice any longer, nothing will be left of my shop."

179

"**You see?**" Beaker moaned. "I should just say that I can't come to accept my award."

"**Wait,**" Bun said. "I'm sorry for losing my temper. Let's start again."

"That would be great," Beaker said as she wiped her face clean with the tablecloth.

Bun snatched the tablecloth away. "**First,**" he said, "never wipe your mouth or face with the tablecloth."

"What should I use?" Beaker asked.

Bun showed her a napkin. "Always use a napkin to keep yourself clean."

"**Oh!**" Beaker said. "I thought that was just a decoration!"

Bun held up a knife and fork. "There are some special foods that you can eat with your hands," Bun said, "but most times, you need to use your knife and fork. If you aren't sure, use a knife and fork just to be safe. They will help you to cut your food into bite-sized pieces. **Watch how I do it.**"

Bun quickly set a fresh table to demonstrate. "It is nice that you wanted to share with me," Bun said as he carefully cut a bite. "But you should never, ever throw food. That is **not good manners**."

"Is there anything else I should know?" Beaker asked.

"Yes," Bun said. "I know that you're a scientist, but the dinner table is no place to do experiments. You should not play with your food."

"I understand," Beaker said with a nod. "I sure made a mess, didn't I? **Let me help you clean up.**"

After Beaker helped Bun clean, she went home to rest for her big dinner the next night.

The next day, she picked out her best dress and went to the banquet.

Beaker shared a table with Posta. "Did Bun help you?" Posta asked.

"He sure did," Beaker replied. "You really know how to deliver."

"Here comes dinner!" Posta said.

Beaker carefully placed her napkin on her lap. "My, this blueberry roast looks wonderful!" She used her fork to taste it.

"What was the experiment that your award is for?" Posta asked. "Could you give me a demonstration?"

"I would," Beaker said, "but the dinner table is no place to play around. I can show you at my lab the next time you come by."

The rest of dinner went smoothly, and soon it was time for Beaker to accept her award. "The most important part of my job is being ready to learn," Beaker said. "So, I would like to thank Bun, because without his teachings, I wouldn't be here tonight."

Everyone at the banquet burst into applause, including Bun, who happily watched his newest student return to her table and finish her meal with excellent manners.

Discussion Questions

Why is it important to use good manners?

Can you think of examples of using good manners that are not mentioned in the story?

MIND YOUR MANNERS

Revised edition. First printing, January 2008.
Copyright 2021 © Lincoln Learning Solutions. All rights reserved.
294 Massachusetts Avenue
Rochester, PA 15074
Visit us on the web at http://www.lincolnlearningsolutions.org.
Midlandia® is a registered trademark of Lincoln Learning Solutions.

Edited by Ashley Mortimer
Character design by Evette Gabriel
Environmental design by Joshua Perry

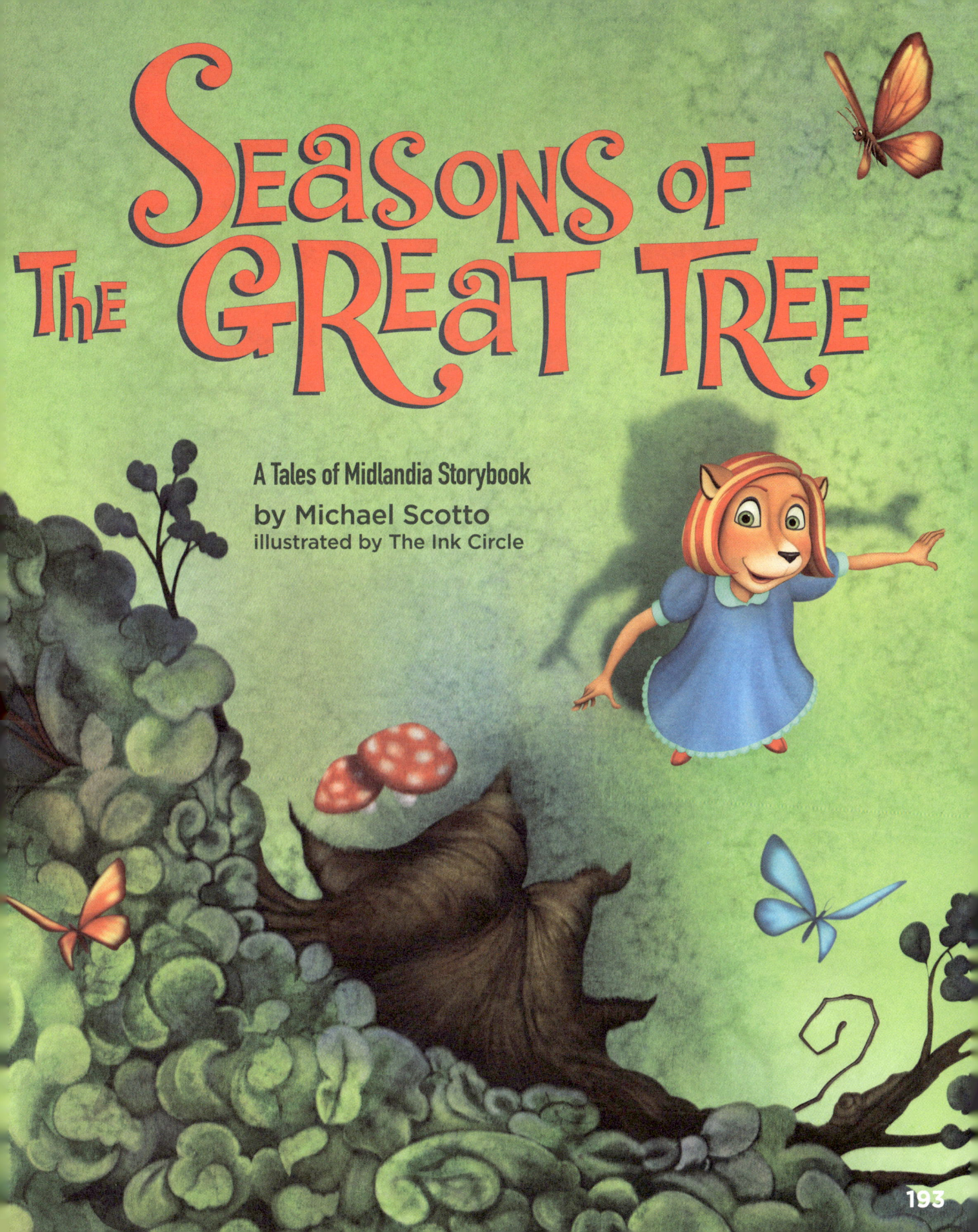

Seasons of the Great Tree

A Tales of Midlandia Storybook

by Michael Scotto
illustrated by The Ink Circle

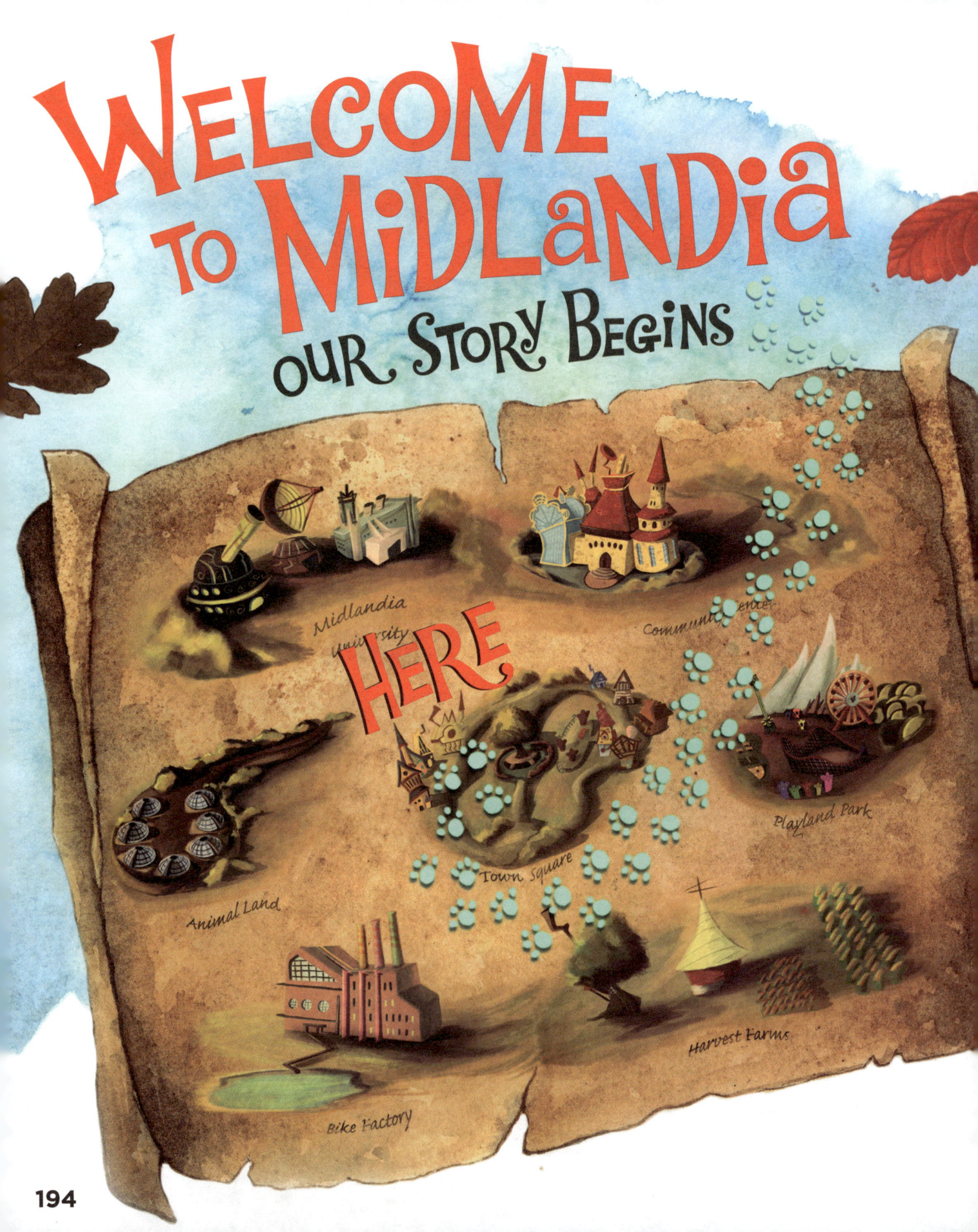

Seasons of the Great Tree

by Michael Scotto
illustrated by The Ink Circle

One afternoon, at the end of summer, Nueva walked past the Great Tree.

I wonder... she thought, *what makes the Great Tree so great?*

Nueva was a reporter for the *Midlandian Times*, and whenever something caught her attention, she wrote about it for the newspaper.

Nueva went to Chief Tatupu, the leader of Midlandia, for answers. "Well, Nueva, the Great Tree is very special," Chief said.

"Long ago, the Great Tree was actually many separate trees. As the years went by, the branches grew together, twisting and turning."

"As the tree limbs wrapped around each other, a single tree began to form, stronger than before. The branches kept working and growing together until they became the Great Tree you see today. They are still working and growing even now!"

"I've never seen it working or growing," Nueva said. "It's always been the same big tree."

"Then perhaps you are not paying enough attention," Chief replied.

Nueva decided that she would do what she always did when something made her curious: She would watch it. She sat down in the shade near the Great Tree with a backpack full of snacks, and she watched.

"I'm not going to leave here until you do something," she told the tree.

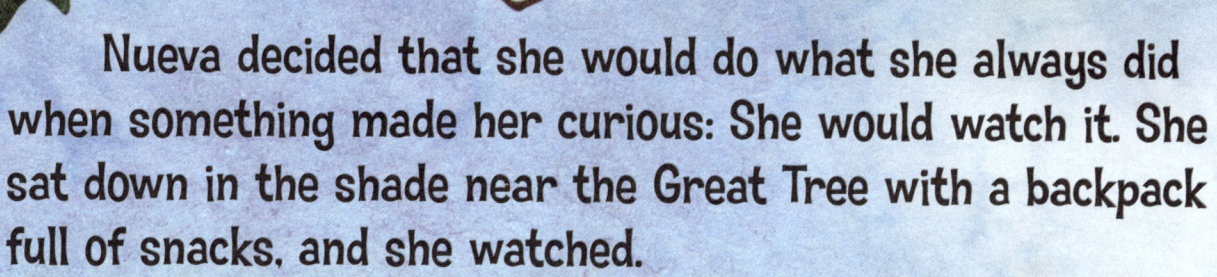

Days passed.
Nueva watched, ate, and wrote in her notebook. "But I can't see you working or growing!" she groaned. Not only that, but she had run out of food. "I'll be back tomorrow, and something had better be different."

The next day, Nueva came back, and something was different. "Your leaves!" she exclaimed. "They're turning yellow! Are you sick?"

"**Chief! Chief!**" Nueva cried, out of breath. She had run all the way from the Great Tree.

"What seems to be the matter?" he asked.

"**Come look!**" she replied.

"It is part of nature," Chief told her, pointing to the tree. "The leaves change every year about this time." And off he went.

But Nueva wasn't sure she believed him. *I'd better keep watching*, she thought.

Nueva visited the Great Tree every day. Soon, the leaves weren't just turning yellow.

"They're turning red, brown, and orange, too!" Nueva said.

Nueva copied every single one in her notebook.

The summer ended and became fall. Now, Nueva had to wear a light jacket when she came to watch the Great Tree. **"How are you feeling today?"** she asked the tree.

The Great Tree then did something very strange: It dropped one of its leaves. The leaf floated to the ground.

Nueva picked up the leaf. Unlike a normal leaf, it was crunchy, not soft. **The tree really is sick**, Nueva thought. *I'd better bring in the professionals.*

The tree shed several more leaves, which fluttered to Nueva's feet.

"**Hurry, Doc,**" Nueva said. "The Great Tree needs your help." Doc Fixit lugged her medical bag after her. "I don't think you understand, Nueva. I take care of Midlandians, not trees."

"**Please, just look?**" Nueva begged.

As Doc looked at the tree, more crunchy leaves fell.

"See, Doc?" Nueva said.

Doc just chuckled. "Oh, Nueva... the Great Tree isn't sick. Its leaves drop off every fall."

"**Don't worry,**" Nueva told the tree. "I'll keep an eye on you just the same."

As fall continued, the leaves piled up, and other Midlandians came to play in them. But Nueva just watched until each branch was bare.

Soon, snow began to fall in Midlandia. Those who didn't have to work came and played at the Great Tree. They threw snowballs, made snow-Midlandians, and played tag around the tree's trunk.

"You don't look very great right now," Nueva told the tree. "You don't look very great at all. You look strange without your leaves," she said. "And how are you keeping warm?"

The next day, Chief found Nueva wrapping blankets around the trunk of the Great Tree. **"What are you doing?"** he asked, astonished.

"Do you have any spare sheets or towels?" she replied. **"I'm all out."**

"Nueva," Chief said, sitting her down. "The Great Tree does not need blankets. In the spring, its leaves will grow back good as new!"

Nueva was doubtful. **"Do you promise?"** she asked.

"I promise," Chief told her. "It happens every year. Just watch."

So, Nueva watched. The new year came, and soon, the snow began to melt off of the Great Tree.

One day, Nueva came to show the tree her new dress. "I'm wearing a new one because I'm too tall for the one I had last spring," she said.

Then, something caught her eye.

"**Green!**" she cried out. It was a single leaf, sprouting from a branch high up on the Great Tree. Every day after, leaves grew back in bunches.

And by the end of the month....

"All of your leaves are back!" Nueva said with excitement. "I have to go find Chief."

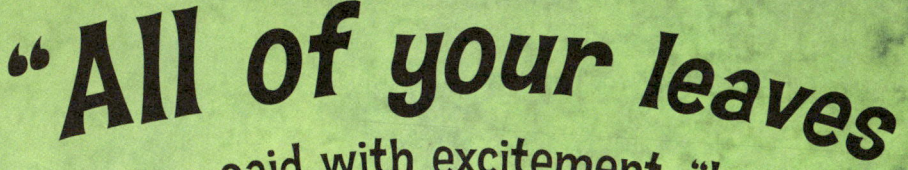

"You were right," Nueva told Chief. "The Great Tree is great again."

"Actually, Nueva," Chief replied, "the Great Tree was always great, even when its leaves were gone."

"All things change all the time. It is a part of life."

"You're right, Chief," Nueva said. "The Great Tree is great because it changes every day. So, the thing that makes it great is the same thing that makes all of us great, too."

Discussion Questions

Change is when something is different today than it used to be.

Can you think of something in your life that has changed?

How are things different?

How do you feel about those changes?

SEASONS OF THE GREAT TREE

Revised edition. First printing, January 2008.
Copyright 2021 © Lincoln Learning Solutions. All rights reserved.
294 Massachusetts Avenue
Rochester, PA 15074
Visit us on the web at http://www.lincolnlearningsolutions.org.
Midlandia® is a registered trademark of Lincoln Learning Solutions.

Edited by Ashley Mortimer
Character design by Evette Gabriel
Environmental design by Joshua Perry

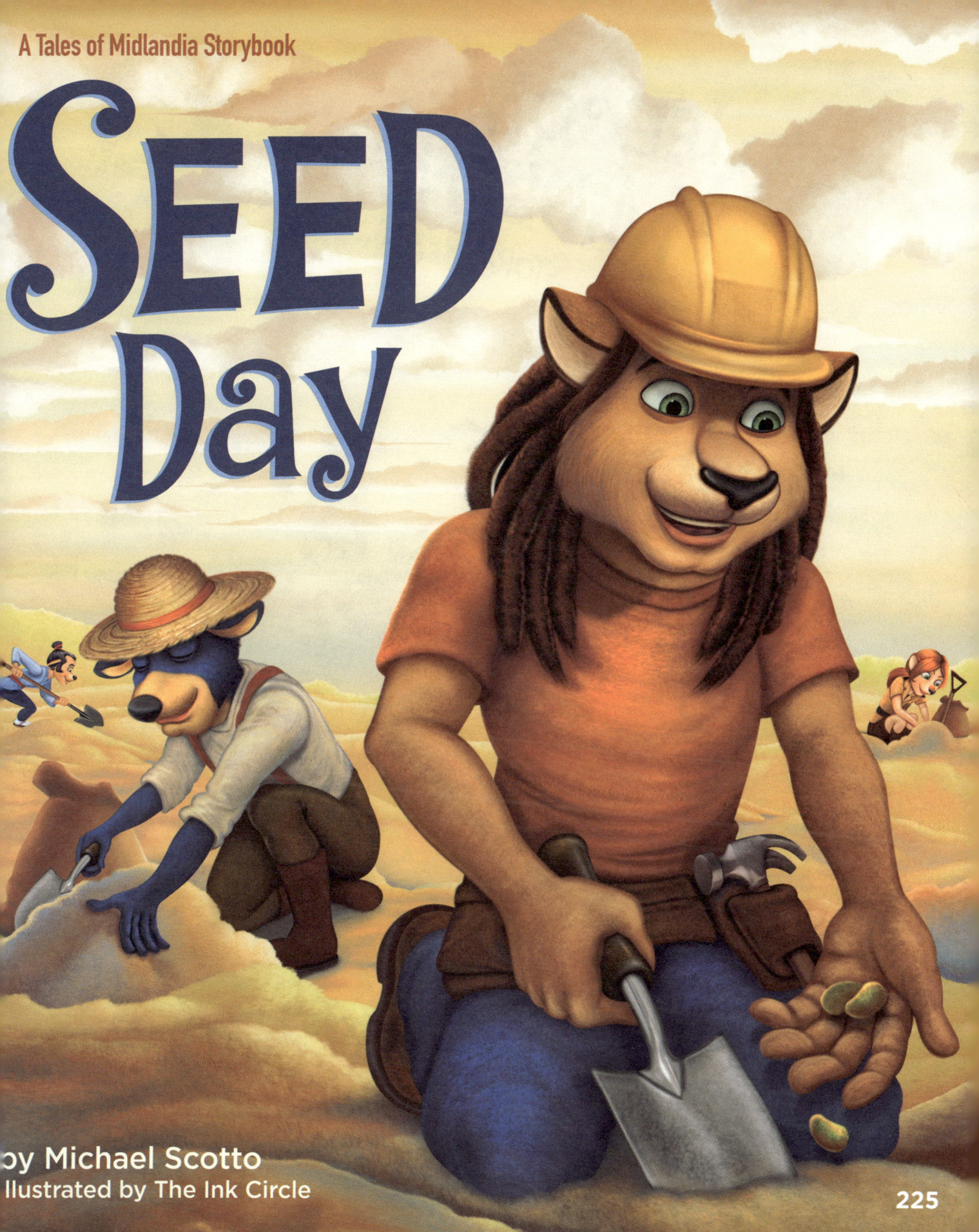

Starring

Brick O. Bobo
The Construction Worker

Seed Day

by Michael Scotto
illustrated by The Ink Circle

Brick O. Bobo loved to visit Tree Town more than any other place in Midlandia. Tree Town was the neighborhood where most Midlandians lived. Brick had built almost every house there. Building was Brick's job. **He was a construction worker.**

Brick did not just build, though. He also fixed buildings when they had problems. Sometimes, he helped Midlandians when they simply wanted a change.

One summer day, Bun the baker invited Brick to his house. "I would like to change my kitchen," said Bun. "The ceiling is too low. When I flip flapjacks for breakfast, they get stuck up there!"

"I'd be happy to help," said Brick. "I'll start later today. First, I need to find some good, strong trees for the job."

With that, Brick headed off for the Midlandia forest.

Most times, it did not take Brick long to find a tall, thick tree to chop. The Midlandia forest was full of them.

At least it used to be. "All I can spot today are stumps!" Brick cried.

Everywhere he walked, Brick found the stumps of trees he had already cut. In some places, there were big brown squares of nothing but stumps.

After a long, sunny hunt, Brick finally found a tree he could use. But he was worried about all those stumpy squares. *It's like the forest is going bald!* he thought.

As he worked in Bun's kitchen, Brick thought about the forest. *What if it runs out of trees?* he wondered. *Where will the birds and the deer live? What will I build with?*

Brick did not have any answers. **He was stumped.**

Soon, Brick finished his work at Bun's house. Bun gave Brick a special thank-you gift.

"Here are some fresh herbs from my garden," said Bun. "Herbs are plants that you can use to flavor your food."

"I can't take your herbs!" cried Brick. "You might run out of them."

"Don't worry," Bun replied with a smile. "I can always plant more."

Bun showed Brick his herb garden. "Each of my herbs starts as a tiny little seed," he explained. "I plant the seed in the soil. With water and sunlight, the seed grows and grows. It is a living thing, just like a plant, flower, or tree."

As Bun spoke, Brick's eyes lit up. He was no longer stumped. He had an idea! But he needed help to make it sprout.

Brick spoke with Chief Tatupu, the leader of Midlandia. He told Chief about the forest, the trees, and the bare, stumpy squares. Chief was shocked. "If we do not do something," he said, **"the forest will end up as bald as me!"**

The next morning, Chief called a special town meeting. He held it in the forest. When everyone had arrived, Brick began to speak. "Every one of us uses trees," he said. "We build our buildings from wood. We turn trees into paper, pencils, and ice-pop sticks."

"The forest has given us so much," Chief added. "Today, it is our turn to give something back. Put on your gardening gloves. Because today...is Seed Day!"

Brick hauled out several huge bags.

"Each of these bags is filled with different seeds," he said. "We have grass seeds and flower seeds... and, of course, lots and lots of tree seeds. If we plant enough in the soil, we can grow a whole new forest."

Brick handed out shovels and handfuls of seeds. **"Let's get started!"**

The Midlandians dug in right away. Dewey and Coach planted grass seeds. Coach imagined the beautiful field they would become.

Sensei and Sparky planted flower seeds in a line. Sensei could picture them growing and blooming.

Antigua tried to plant something very odd.
"**Help!**" cried Buck. "**She's trying to plant me!**"
"Maybe it'll help you grow!" she said, laughing.
"Now, now," said Chief. "Midlandians grow differently than plants. Besides, Buck is the perfect height as he is."

All the while, Brick and some others planted trees. They planted seed after seed all day long. *I can't wait to see this forest grow,* thought Brick.

Finally, the sun began to set. The Midlandians were very proud of their work. "What a smashing Seed Day!" said Broadway the actor.

"Yes, it was," Brick agreed. "But our work is not done." Several Midlandians were puzzled.

"It's not?" they asked.

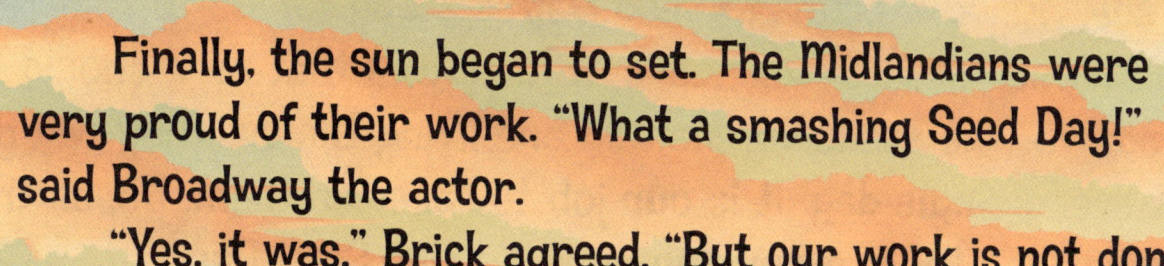

"You see," Brick explained, "Seed Day is a day for us to think about nature and do our best to take care of it. But all that care should not end at sundown. The seeds we planted are living things. They will grow a little bit every single day. It is our job to care for them. So, as this forest grows, let's treat every day as if it were Seed Day."

Discussion Questions

What is your favorite kind of plant?
Do you have any plants at home? What kinds?

There are some things that living things must have to survive. These things are called basic needs. What are plants' basic needs? What are animals' basic needs? How do you get your basic needs?

Why is it important to take care of nature?
What are some ways that you can help?

SEED DAY

Revised edition. First printing, January 2011.
Copyright 2021 © Lincoln Learning Solutions. All rights reserved.
294 Massachusetts Avenue
Rochester, PA 15074
Visit us on the web at http://www.lincolnlearningsolutions.org.
Midlandia® is a registered trademark of Lincoln Learning Solutions.

Edited by Ashley Mortimer
Character design by Evette Gabriel
Environmental design by Joshua Perry

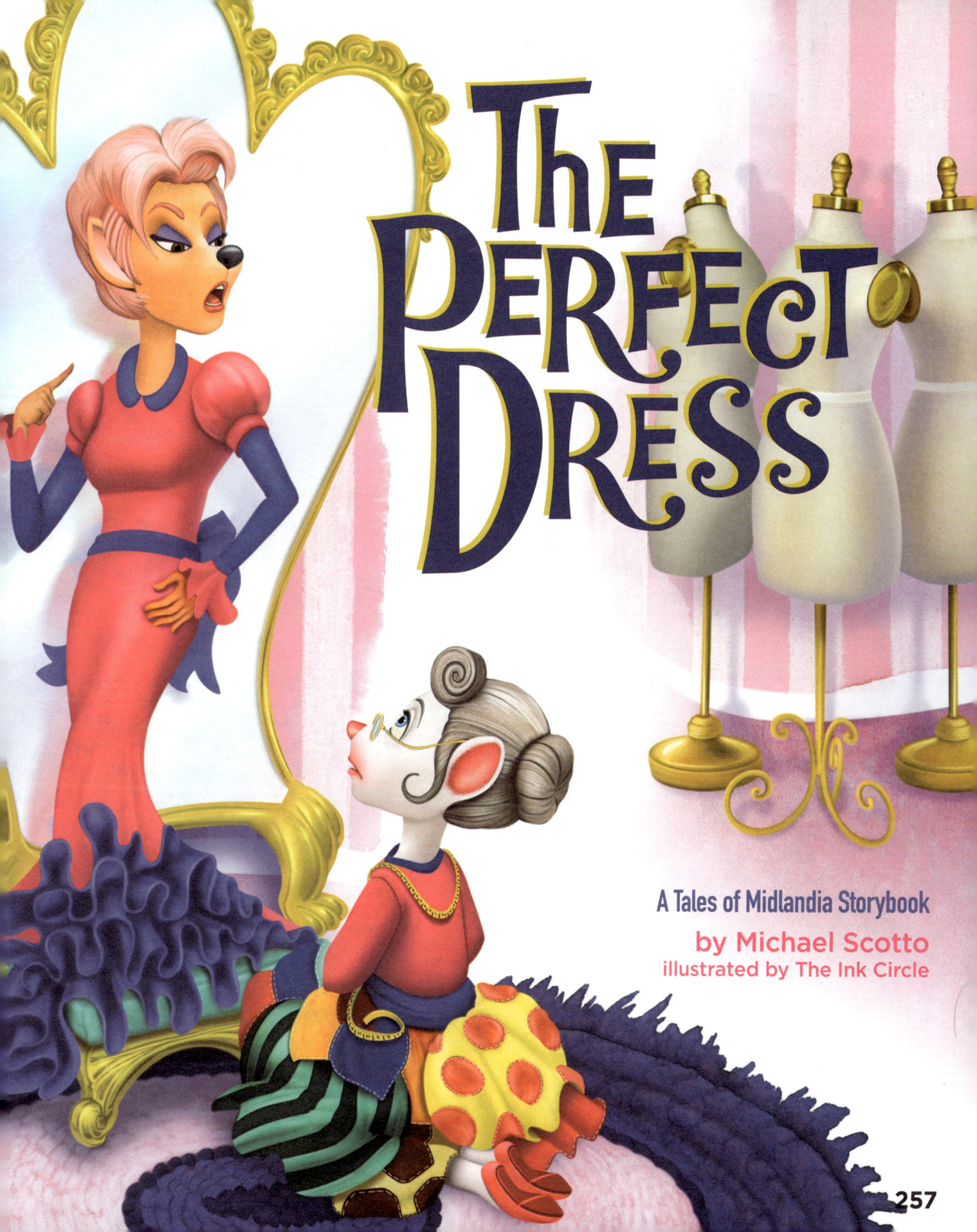

The Perfect Dress

A Tales of Midlandia Storybook

by Michael Scotto
illustrated by The Ink Circle

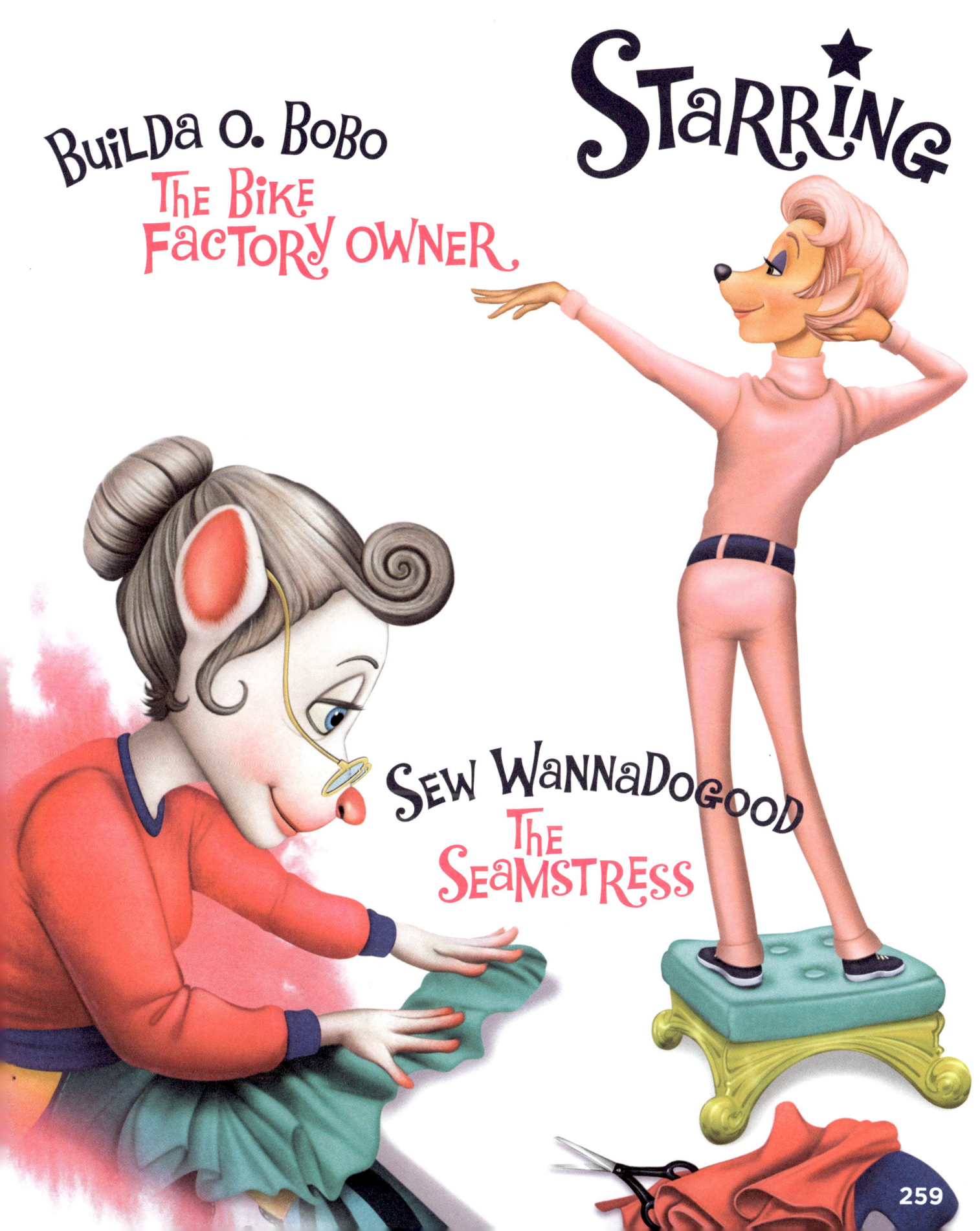

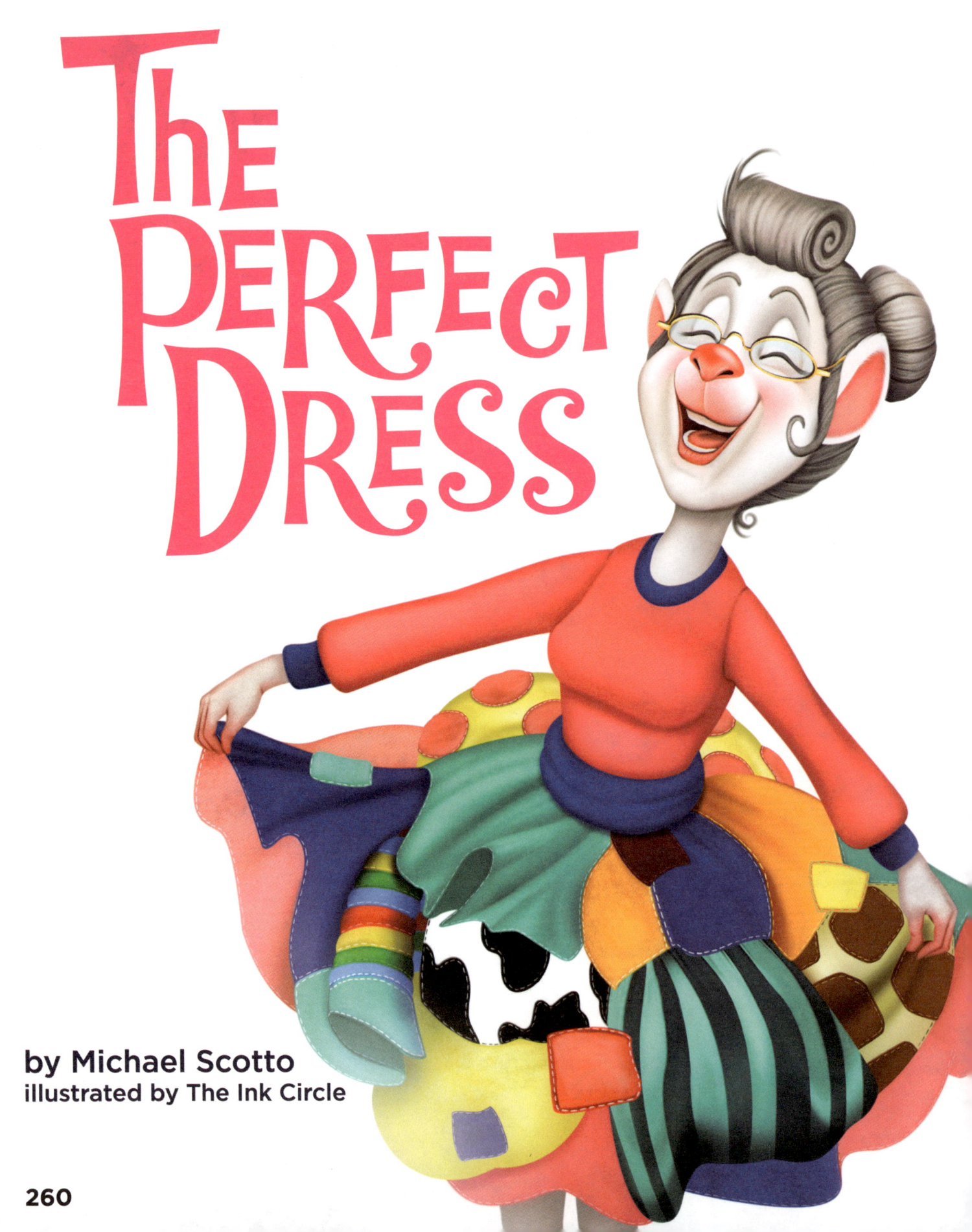

The Perfect Dress

by Michael Scotto
illustrated by The Ink Circle

Sew was the seamstress for all of Midlandia. She mended clothes that were torn, and she made new clothing, too.

The dress Sew wore was very special. She had taken the leftover bits of cloth from each thing she had ever made and put them together to make something colorful.

Each piece reminded Sew of each person she had helped.

One morning, Builda hurried into Sew's shop. Builda owned a bicycle factory in town, and she was always in a rush.

"Good morning, Builda," Sew said. "What brings you here today?"

Builda quickly checked her clipboard. "Well," she replied, "first, I cleaned my house from top to bottom. Then, I had a quick morning workout with my pal Sensei. And now, I am here because I need a new dress."

Sew was a little puzzled. "But didn't I make you a new dress just last month?"

"Well, yes," Builda said. "But that dress was for a dinner party, and now I'm going to a dinner dance. **I need something new.**"

"Okay..." Sew said as she took a measurement. "If you insist. What kind of dress would you like?"

"I want it exactly like the last one," Builda said. "Only, put some pink ruffles on the sleeves this time."

"Come back in a week," Sew said, "and your dress will be ready."

Builda checked her list. "Oh, my!" she cried. "I wasted all this time talking to you, and now I'm going to be late to the factory!" And with that, Builda dashed off.

Sew **worked** and **cut** and **stitched** for a whole week until, finally, she thought Builda's new dress was perfect.

But when Builda returned....

"What do you mean?" Sew asked.

"All I mean," Builda said, "is that I am a stylish Midlandian, and I can't be seen wearing the kind of clothes that you wear. **Okay?**"

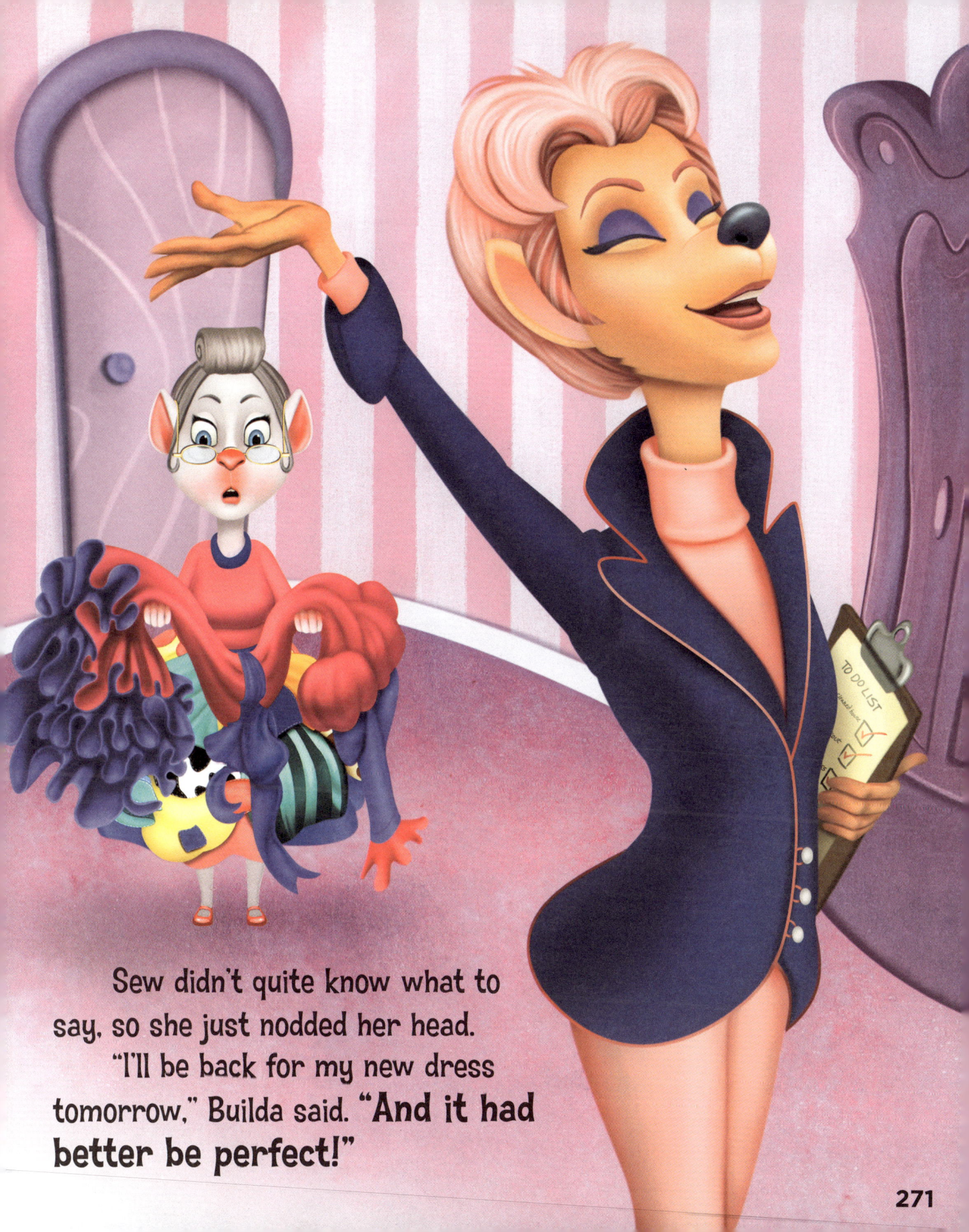

Sew didn't quite know what to say, so she just nodded her head.

"I'll be back for my new dress tomorrow," Builda said. "And it had better be perfect!"

Sew didn't know much about fancy clothes, but she knew she could learn about them at the library.

"You're here late," Dewey said. Dewey was a librarian. He helped all the Midlandians who came to the library find what they needed.

"Do you have any books on fancy dresses?" Sew asked.

Dewey helped Sew find lots of books full of pictures of pretty dresses. *But I have no idea which one is perfect!* Sew thought. She became very worried.

"Are you all right, Sew?" Dewey asked.

"I just don't know what to do!" Sew moaned. "Builda wants the perfect dress, but I don't know if I can cut it!"

"But Sew, everyone loves your clothes," Dewey said. "Why are you worried?"

Sew hung her head. "Builda said that my dress was a bunch of shabby rags," she whispered.

"That was not a nice thing for her to say," Dewey told her. "It's okay if Builda does not like the clothes that you wear, but she should not tease you about them. The important thing is that your clothes are perfect for you."

"You're right, Dewey," Sew said. "I feel a little better."
"That's what the D-Man is here for!" he replied.

Sew worked through the night, but it was just not enough time to finish a whole new dress. In the morning, Builda rushed into Sew's shop. "Where is my dress?" Builda demanded.

"One day wasn't enough time to finish it," Sew said. "I can show you what I have."

When Builda saw the dress, she turned bright red! "Maybe you like wearing half a dress," she cried, **"but I need a whole one!"**

Sew had had enough! "The way you are talking to me isn't very nice," she said. "If you can't start being nice, I can't finish your dress for you."

Builda was stunned. **"What do you mean?"** she asked. **"I'm very nice."**

"No," Sew replied. "You were not nice yesterday when you said my dress was shabby."

"But look at it," Builda said. "It's just a bunch of scraps."

"**It might look like a bunch of scraps to you,**" Sew said, "but each piece means something to me. Every time I make new clothes, I save a little piece of the cloth and add it to my dress. That way, I never forget all the people I've helped."

Sew showed Builda a little square at the bottom of her dress. "This is from the dress I made for you last month. You might not think that it's fancy enough, but every scrap is special to me."

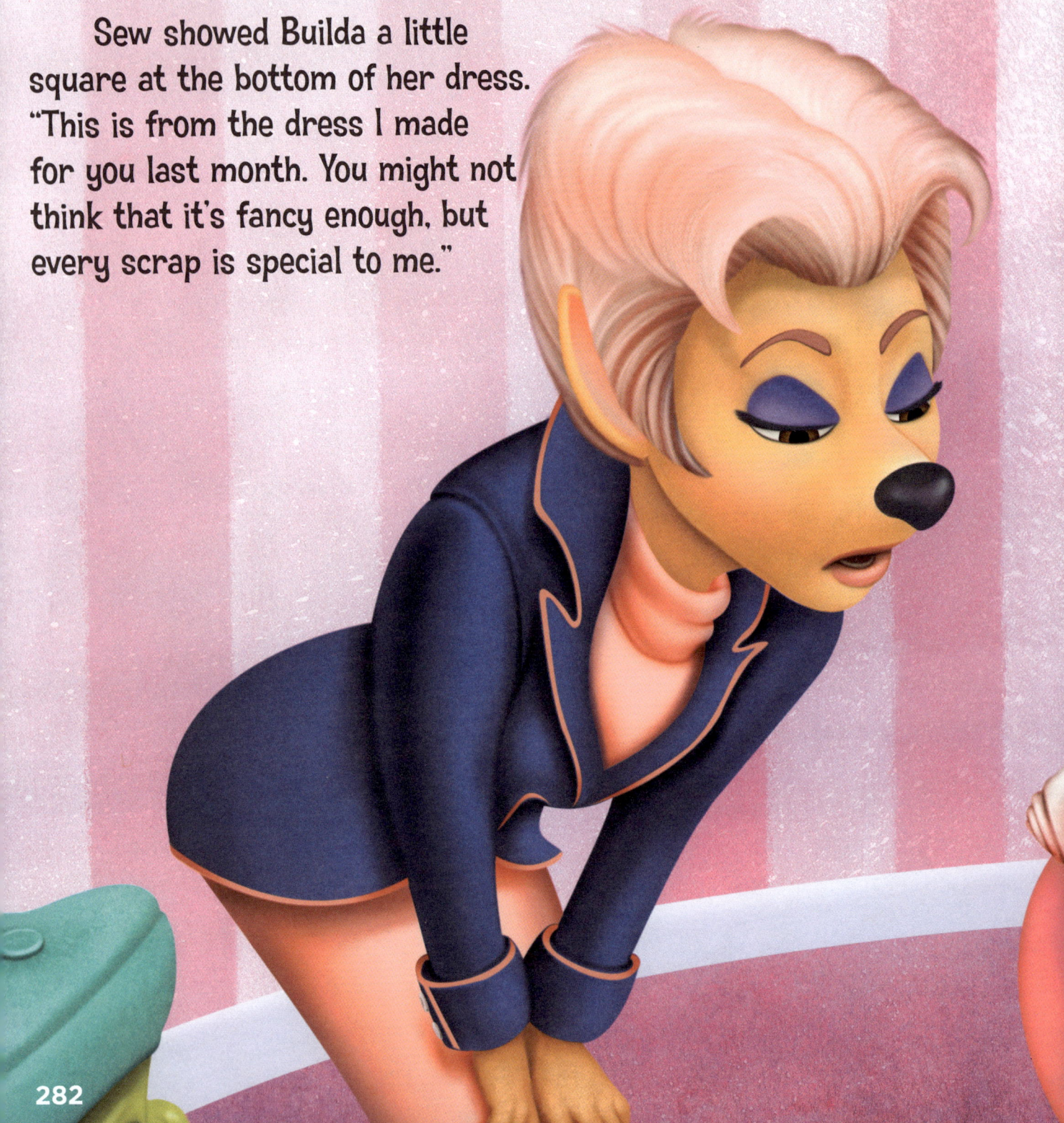

"I didn't realize what your dress meant to you," Builda said. "But now that I know, **I'm really sorry for calling it shabby.** And I'd love it if you would come with me to the dinner dance and wear it there."

"I'd love to!" Sew said.

The next evening, the two friends went together to the dance, and everybody admired Sew's handiwork. The two dresses were very different, but each one was a perfect fit.

Discussion Questions

Which dress did you like better, Builda's or Sew's? Why?

In the story, was Builda a bully? Why was she wrong?

What should you do if someone bullies you?

THE PERFECT DRESS

Revised edition. First printing, January 2008.
Copyright 2021 © Lincoln Learning Solutions. All rights reserved.
294 Massachusetts Avenue
Rochester, PA 15074
Visit us on the web at http://www.lincolnlearningsolutions.org.
Midlandia® is a registered trademark of Lincoln Learning Solutions.

Edited by Ashley Mortimer
Character design by Evette Gabriel
Environmental design by Joshua Perry

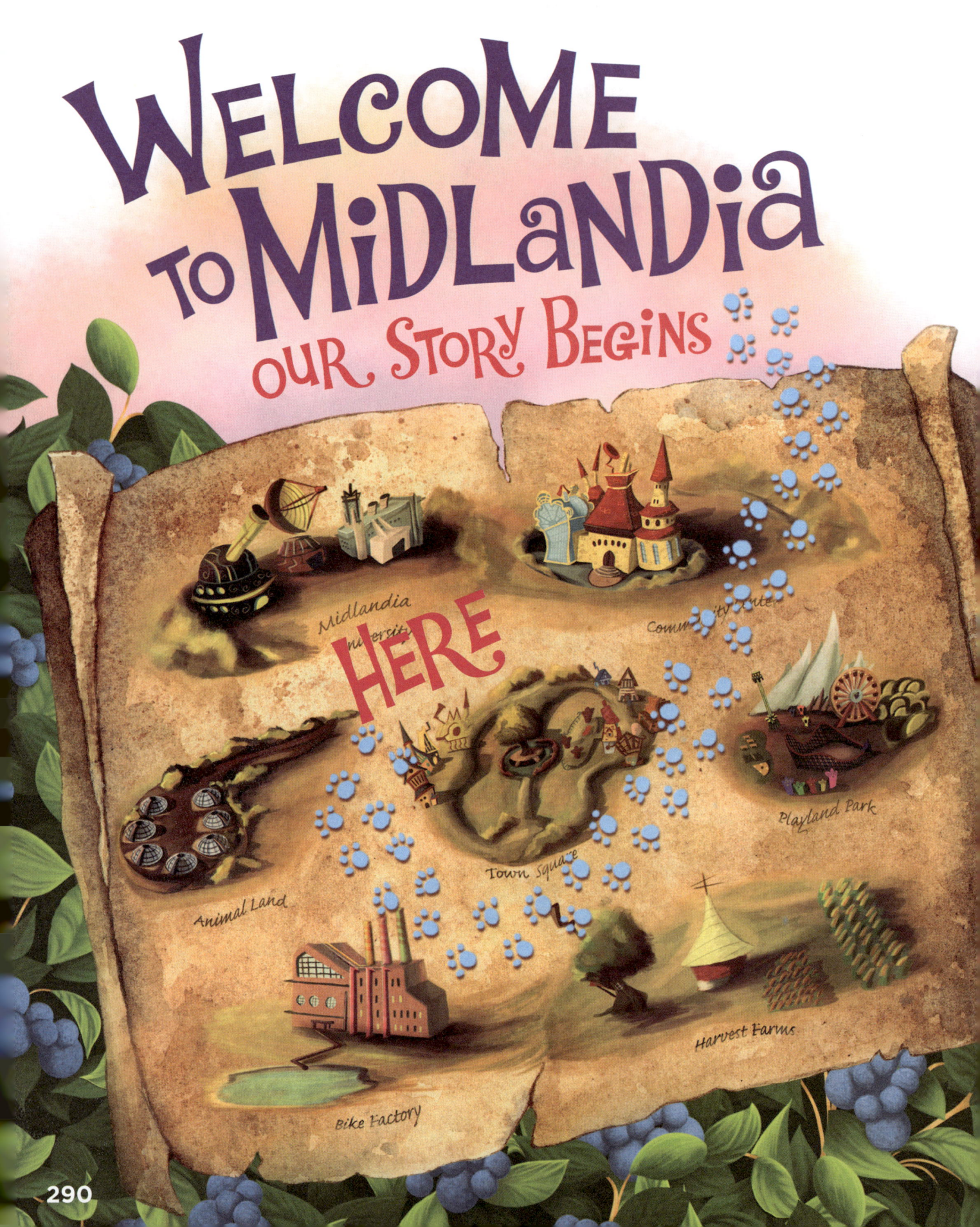

The Pride of Midlandia

by Michael Scotto
illustrated by The Ink Circle

No more ice, and no more snow. Spring had finally come! The flowers bloomed, and the blueberries grew. All of Midlandia was abuzz and aflutter. It was a lively and happy time.

Not every Midlandian was happy, though. Sheriff Badge was nervous. "**Why, oh why, did Chief pick me?**" she wondered.

Chief Tatupu was the leader of Midlandia. He had given Badge a very big and very special job.

Each spring, the Midlandians held a parade. The parade celebrated all of the good things about Midlandia.

"I would like for you to make a parade float," Chief told Badge. "A float is a special kind of stage. It has wheels so that it can be pulled along during the parade. Your float should show why you are proud to be a Midlandian."

Badge loved Midlandia. There were so many things about it that made her proud. But there was one problem. **How can I fit it all onto one little float?** she thought.

Badge went to see Vincent van Wannadogood for advice. Vincent was a Midlandian artist. His paintings were known all over the world.

"If I showed everything that made me proud," said Badge, "I'd need a float the size of our whole town!"

Vincent stroked his beard. "Why not pick the one thing that makes you proudest?" he suggested. "Just look around Midlandia. When you find the right idea for your float, you will feel it. And when you're ready, I'll help you build it!"

Badge was happy to have Vincent's help. *But first,* she thought, *I need an idea!*

Badge started her search in the Town Square. She visited some Midlandians who were preparing for the parade.

Sew the seamstress was working in her shop. She was stitching a new Midlandian flag. The flag was a symbol of Midlandia. "I'm going to carry it at the front of the parade!" Sew told Badge. **"It will be so beautiful."**

Outside, Badge found Harmony. Harmony was a musician. She was practicing with her band. **"Play it loud, play it proud!"** said Harmony. The band marched and played the Midlandian national anthem. It was a song about the traditions of Midlandia.

Badge thought about the flag and the anthem as she walked on. "They're both very important," she said to herself. "But they're already going to be in the parade. I need something different."

Next, Badge walked over to Animal Land. That was the zoo in Midlandia. She was very proud to have it in her town. Wilda the zookeeper greeted Badge at the gates. "You need a float?" asked Wilda. **"Check this out!"**

Wilda showed Badge some small furry animals splashing and floating in a stream.

"Meet my friends, the sea otters," said Wilda. "The sea otter is the national animal of Midlandia. Sea otters are perfect for a float. **They float all day!**"

Badge helped Wilda feed the sea otters some fish. "They do like to float," Badge agreed. "But I don't know if they're right for my float."

Badge exited Animal Land. *I still haven't found the right idea,* she thought. *Maybe Chief made a mistake trusting me.*

Badge wandered over the hills and ended up near Harvest Farms. Harvest the farmer was picking blueberries in his field. *Blueberries are our most popular food*, thought Badge. *But how can I make a blueberry float?*

Badge saw that Harvest was not alone. Captain Koostoe was there, too. He took Harvest's blueberries to distant lands on his ship. But today, he was not shipping. **He was picking!**

"Thanks for helping me, Koostoe," said Harvest. "You really did not have to offer. It's not your job to pick blueberries."

"Four hands are always better than two," replied Koostoe. "Now we can finish early and share a glass of lemonade together."

As she watched, Badge felt very proud of Koostoe. She loved how Midlandians always helped each other. **And then she realized....**

"**I found my idea!**" Badge told Vincent. She described the float she had in mind.

Vincent smiled. "That sounds wonderful!" he said. "I'll round up a team and get to work. We'll need Brick the builder, some bike wheels from Builda, flowers from Sensei's garden...."

Badge, Vincent, and their friends worked together on the float. By the day before the parade, it was ready!

Badge showed the float to Chief Tatupu. "The blueberry bush stands for food, one of our basic needs," she explained. "The hands are working as a team to hold the bush up. They are like us Midlandians. We work together to provide basic needs for everyone."

Chief smiled. "This is perfect for our parade!" he said. "I knew you would come through."

"How did you know to pick me?" asked Badge.

"You are a police officer, which means it is your job to protect Midlandia," answered Chief. "I thought that you would know best why Midlandia is worth protecting."

Badge blushed.

"I just have one more favor to ask of you," said Chief. "Would you ride on this float with me tomorrow?" Badge turned an even deeper red.

The next day was parade day. Sew's flag flapped in the wind. Harmony's band marched and played. Chief and Badge followed in the back. They waved to the crowd. And as she stood on the float that so many friends helped to make, Badge felt **proud to be a Midlandian.**

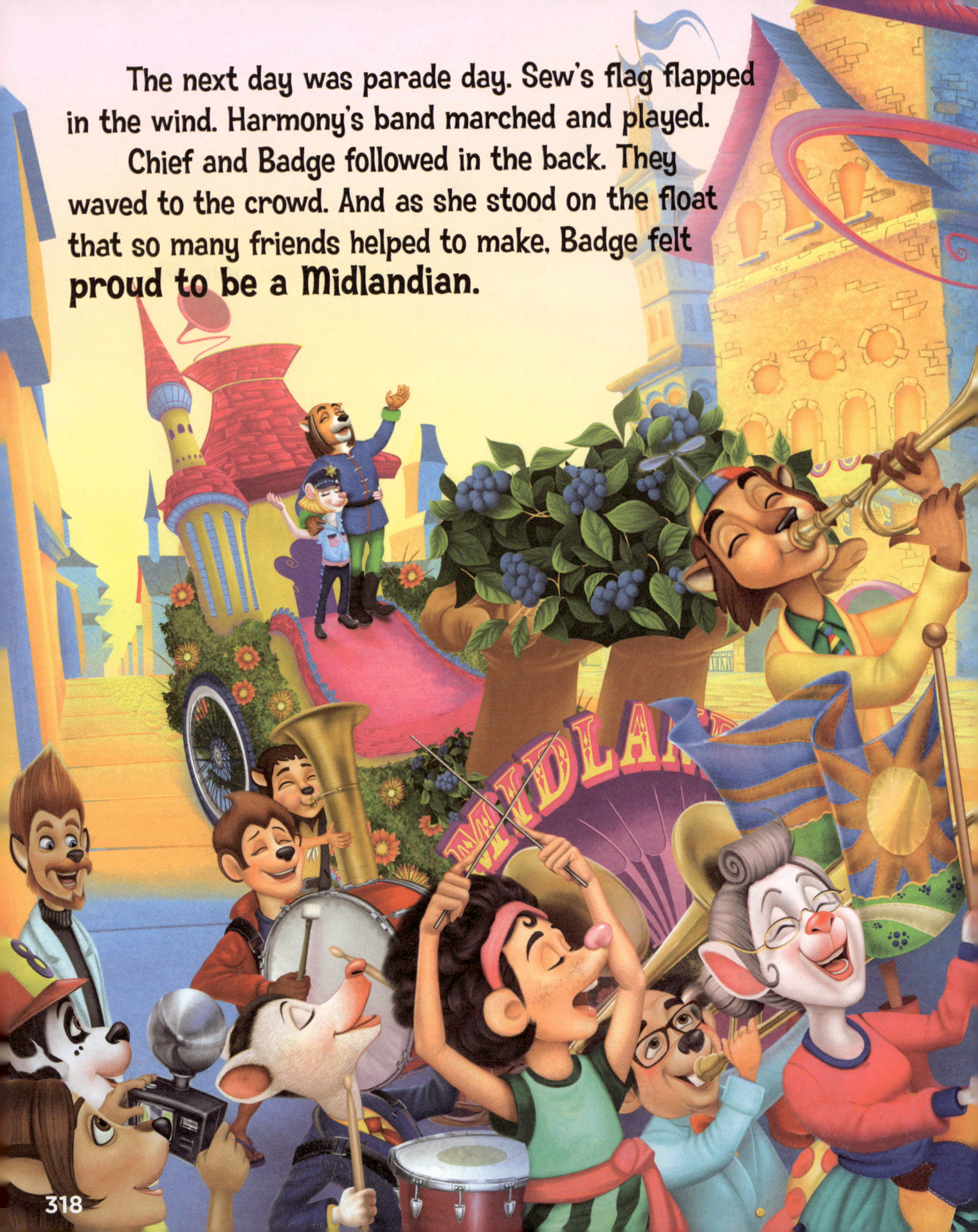

Discussion Questions

Can you think of any symbols for your country?
What does your country's flag look like?

A tradition is something that a group of people does year after year.
The parade in Midlandia is a tradition.
Does your family celebrate any traditions?

THE PRIDE OF MIDLANDIA

Revised edition. First printing, January 2010.
Copyright 2021 © Lincoln Learning Solutions. All rights reserved.
294 Massachusetts Avenue
Rochester, PA 15074
Visit us on the web at http://www.lincolnlearningsolutions.org.
Midlandia® is a registered trademark of Lincoln Learning Solutions.

Edited by Ashley Mortimer
Character design by Evette Gabriel
Environmental design by Joshua Perry

Wilda's General Store Adventure

A Tales of Midlandia Storybook
by Michael Scotto
Illustrated by The Ink Circle

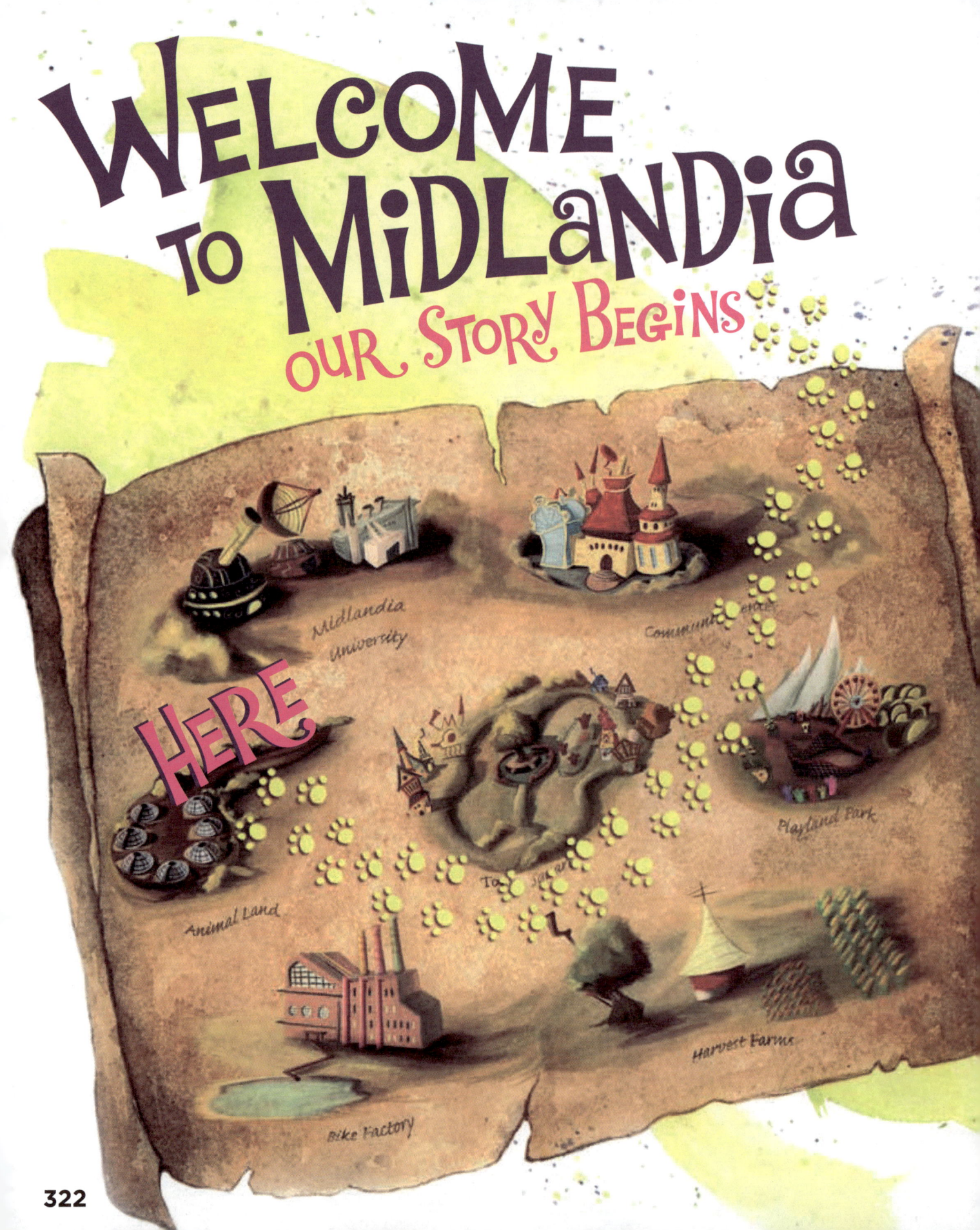

Wilda's General Store Adventure

by Michael Scotto
illustrated by The Ink Circle

Wilda was the zookeeper of Animal Land in Midlandia. Her job was to make sure the tigers, monkeys, giraffes, and other animals that lived there were well-fed and had plenty of space to roam.

Every week, Wilda shopped for food at the Midlandia General Store.

Wilda always tried to get the animals' favorite foods.

"Bananas for the monkeys, peanuts for the elephants, carrots for the zebras, and apples for the giraffes...."

If she couldn't find something she wanted, she would politely ask Scannit for help. "Excuse me…can you tell me where I can find the Brussels sprouts? Larry the lion loves Brussels sprouts!"

"Go to aisle seven," Scannit said. "You'll find them right by the apples." Scannit owned the General Store. He knew just as much about his store as Wilda did about her zoo.

It took Wilda most of the afternoon to find the favorite food of each animal. *I'd better get back soon,* Wilda thought. *The chinchillas are afraid of the dark.*

It was an Ink!

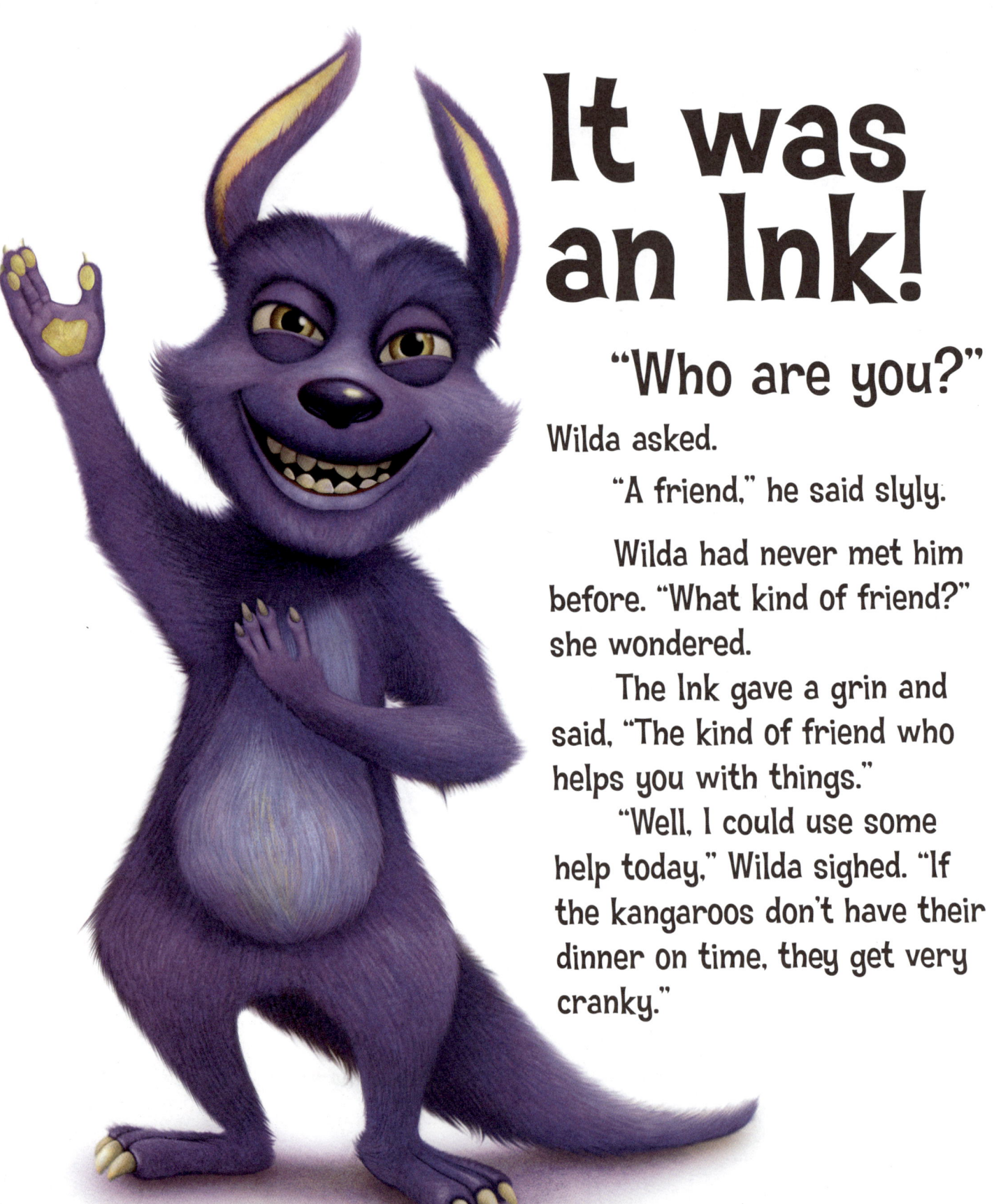

"Who are you?" Wilda asked.

"A friend," he said slyly.

Wilda had never met him before. "What kind of friend?" she wondered.

The Ink gave a grin and said, "The kind of friend who helps you with things."

"Well, I could use some help today," Wilda sighed. "If the kangaroos don't have their dinner on time, they get very cranky."

The Ink scurried closer. "I know what you can do," he whispered. "Just walk out the door."

"You think I should leave without paying?" Wilda exclaimed. **"Shhh, not so loud,"** the Ink said. "If you're in a hurry, Scannit won't mind. Just skip past the line and run home."

"Well," Wilda replied, "it would help me save some time...." **"Then hurry up!"** said the Ink, and he tossed a box of powdered sugar on the floor, where it burst open in a cloud of dust

"Oh!" cried Wilda. "I'm not sure you should be doing that."
"I can do whatever I want!"
He flopped on his back and made a powdered sugar angel.
"The supermarket sure is fun!" he said.

But then a voice came from the end of the aisle. "Whoa! Hold on there, little partner!"

Wilda hurried to Scannit, her face red with embarrassment. "Scannit, I'm glad you're here! I wasn't sure what to do." She pointed to the Ink. "He was saying I should leave without paying."

Scannit leaned over the Ink as the rascal dusted himself off. "Is that true?" Scannit asked.

The Ink looked from side to side.
"Um...I have to go now."

The Ink kicked up a cloud of sugar and dashed away.

"Those critters are always causing trouble," Scannit said as he mopped up the sugar.

"I'm so confused," Wilda said. "Can you tell me what I should do?"

"At the supermarket," Scannit explained, "you have to get in line and wait your turn. If someone gets in line before you, it's only fair that they go first, even if you're in a hurry."

Wilda took her place in line and waited for her turn.

At the checkout counter, Scannit picked up each item from Wilda's cart. "Thanks for waiting," Scannit said. He used his scanner to find out how much each item cost. "You have to pay for each item you pick out," he said. "So, I check each one to make sure I don't charge you too much or too little."

After paying her bill, Wilda said, "I'd better get home before the monkeys make a mess. Since you were such a big help, next time you come to Animal Land, I'll give you a tour!"

"No trouble at all, ma'am," Scannit said as he waved goodbye.

Back at Animal Land, Wilda served dinner. The monkeys clapped, the kangaroos hopped, the chinchillas chirped...and that night, the whole zoo went to sleep with full, happy bellies.

Discussion Questions

What is your favorite food to buy at the grocery store?

How do you feel when someone cuts in line?

Do you think it is wrong to take something and not pay for it? Why?

WILDA'S GENERAL STORE ADVENTURE

Revised edition. First printing, January 2008.
Copyright 2020 © Lincoln Learning Solutions. All rights reserved.
294 Massachusetts Avenue
Rochester, PA 15074
Visit us on the web at http://www.lincolnlearningsolutions.org.
Midlandia® is a registered trademark of Lincoln Learning Solutions.

Edited by Ashley Mortimer
Character design by Evette Gabriel
Environmental design by Joshua Perry